DATE			

Five Plays by Ed Bullins

Five Plays by Ed Bullins

Goin' a Buffalo

In the Wine Time

A Son, Come Home

The Electronic Nigger

Clara's Ole Man

The Bobbs-Merrill Company
Indianapolis and New York

Goin' a Buffalo first appeared in *New Black Playwrights*, William Couch, ed., copyright © 1969 Louisiana State University Press. A Son, Come Home was first published in the April 1968 issue of *The Negro Digest*. Clara's Ole Man was first published in the Summer 1968 issue of *The Drama Review*, and The Electronic Nigger first appeared in *New American Plays, Vol. 3*, William M. Hoffman, ed., copyright © 1969 by Hill & Wang, Inc.

The Bobbs-Merrill Company, Inc.
A Subsidiary of Howard W. Sams & Co., Inc.
Publishers/Indianapolis • Kansas City • New York

To my mother...
Bertha Marie Bullins.
Who taught me
to
read & write/rite.

CONTENTS

Helen Ellis, George Miles and Crystal Field in a scene from Goin' a Buffalo. *(Pho⟨ by Martha Holmes, courtesy of The American Place Theatre.)*

GOIN' A BUFFALO

A Tragifantasy

Sometimes . . .
I'd like to be
a Stranger in town . . .
Sort'a mysterious.
Strange tales would be
told about me . . .
And they would be
Fantastic!
    Martin P. Abramson

Goin' a Buffalo was presented as a staged reading at the American Place Theatre on the evenings of June 6th and 7th, 1968. It was directed by Roscoe Orman. The production stage manager was Peter Galambos, Gary Bolling was the stage manager, David Jacobs designed the lighting and the electrician was Owen Ryan. The cast was as follows:

CURT, 29 years old	Kris Keiser
RICH, 28 years old	Ed Smith
PANDORA, 22 years old, Curt's wife	Helen Ellis
ART, 23 years old	George Miles
MAMMA TOO TIGHT, 20 years old	Crystal Field
SHAKY, 36 years old. Mamma Too Tight's man	Whitman Mayo
PIANO PLAYER	Buddy Davis
BASS PLAYER	Bill Lathan
DRUMMER	Ed Smith
BARTENDER	Bob Johnson
DEENY	Ed Madson
BOUNCER	George Fairley
A CUSTOMER	Ed Madson
SHOWGIRL	Yvette Hawkins
VOICE	

SYNOPSIS OF SCENES

ACT ONE: Evening.
ACT TWO: Later that evening.
ACT THREE: Three days later.

The action of the play takes place in Curt's apartment and at the Strip Club.

ACT I

SCENE 1

This play is about some black people: CURT, PANDORA, ART, RICH and SHAKY, though MAMMA TOO TIGHT is white. The remainder of the cast is interracial, but two of the MUSICIANS are black and if DEENY, the BOUNCER, and one of the CUSTOMERS are white, there might be added tensions. But it is left to the director's imagination to match the colors to the portrayals.

Time: Early 1960's, late evening in January.

Scene: A court apartment in Los Angeles in the West Adams district. The room is done in white: white ceiling, white walls, white overly elaborate furniture; but a red wall-to-wall carpet covers the floor. A wall bed is raised. Upstage, two doorless entrances stand on each side of the head of the bed. The right entrance is to the kitchen; the rear stage area that represents the kitchen is shielded by a filmy curtain and the actors' dim silhouettes are seen when the area is lighted. The left entrance will be raised and offstage right at the head of a short flight of stairs and a platform which leads into the combination bathroom–dressing room–closet. When the actors are within this area their shadows will be cast upon the wall fronting the stairs. And when the bed is lowered a scarlet spread is shown.

3

Within the interior of the front room the light is a mixture of red, blues, and violet, with crimson shadows bordering the edges of the stage to create the illusion of a world afire, with this pocket of atmosphere an oasis.

A Telefunken, turned very low, plays the local jazz station, and CURT and RICH lean over a chessboard. CURT squats upon a stool, and facing him across the coffee table and chessboard, RICH, a stocky, brooding man, studies his next move, seated on the edge of the couch. Each has an empty beer bottle and a glass close at hand.

CURT
I just about have you up tight, Rich.

RICH *(Annoyed)*
Aww ... Curt, man ... don't try and hustle me!

CURT *(Looks at him)*
Did I say somethin' to upset you, man?

(RICH *shakes his head and curses to himself.*

A shadow appears at head of stairs and pauses as if the figure is listening for conversation, then PANDORA *enters, a beautiful black girl wearing tight white pants, a crimson blouse and black boots, and slowly descends the stairs while looking at the men. She crosses behind them and walks toward the kitchen.* RICH *looks a second at her behind, but drops his gaze when* CURT *begins tapping the chessboard with a fingernail.* CURT *gives no discernible attention to* PANDORA. *She enters the kitchen; a light goes on)*

CURT *(Staring at RICH)*
This game's somethin' else ... man.

RICH *(Studies board, looks up at* CURT *and concentrates upon the board again. Mutters to himself)*
Ain't this somethin' else, though . . .
        (Looking up)
You almost got my ass, man.

CURT *(Mocking)*
I have got your ass, Rich.

RICH *(Half-hearted)*
Aww . . . man . . . why don't you go fuck yourself?
        (He places hand upon a piece)

CURT *(Warning and placing hand upon one of his pieces)*
Wouldn't do that if I were you, good buddy.

RICH *(Frowns and takes hand from board; he shakes head and mumbles, then curses his own caution)*
Sheeet!
        (He makes move)
Let's see what you're goin' ta do with that, man!

CURT *(Deliberately)*
Checkmate!

RICH *(Half-rising)*
What you say, Curt?

CURT *(Toneless)*
Checkmate, man.
        (CURT *looks toward the rear of the apartment; the faucet has been turned on, and in the kitchen* PANDORA *leisurely crosses the entrance doorway)*
We're ready for another one, Pandora!

PANDORA *(Off)*
Already!

CURT
That's what I said, baby!

PANDORA *(Re-crosses doorway)*
Okay.

RICH *(Mumbles and studies chessboard)*
Well . . . I'll be goddamned.

> *(Faucet sound goes off)*

PANDORA *(Off)*
You don't need fresh glasses, do ya?

> *(Sound of refrigerator opening)*

CURT *(Surly)*
No, Pandora, just the beer!

PANDORA *(Raising voice)*
Okay . . . okay . . . wait a fuckin' minute, will ya? Be
right there!

> *(Rattle of bottles)*

CURT *(Glowering toward the kitchen, then staring at
        RICH, who sits stoop-shouldered)*
How 'bout another one, Rich?

> (RICH *reaches into pocket and brings out a
> small roll and pulls off two bills and places them
> beside* CURT's *glass. He mutters to himself)*

RICH
I wonder why in the fuck I didn't see that?

PANDORA *(With a cross expression enters carrying
        two bottles of Miller's High Life)*
Just because you're pissed off at the world, don't
take it out on me! What ta hell ya think ya got 'round
here, maid service?

> (CURT *stands to meet her; she slows.*
>
> *Whining)*

Aww . . . Curt . . .

> *(A knock comes from backstage; relieved, she
> looks at* CURT)

6   GOIN' A BUFFALO

I wonder who would be knocking at the kitchen door, honey?

CURT *(Reaches down, palms and pockets the money)*
There's only one way to be sure, sugar.

    (Sits down, looks at RICH*)*
You clean, man?

RICH *(Nods)*
Yeah . . . Curt.

CURT *(Nods to* PANDORA *as the knock sounds again)*
Just watch your mouth, pretty baby . . . it's goin' ta get you in trouble one of these days, ya know.

    (PANDORA *places bottles on the edge of the table and briskly goes to open back door)*

PANDORA
Maybe it's Little Mamma already.

CURT *(Mostly to himself)*
She wouldn't come around to the back door for nobody.
    (CURT *disregards the noise of the kitchen door's lock snapping back and the rattle of the night chain being fixed in its hasp)*
I have the black men this time, right, Rich?

RICH *(Reaching for the beer)*
Yeah.

ART *(Off)*
Hello, is Curt home? My name's Art. I ran into Curt this afternoon and he told me to drop by.

PANDORA *(Off)*
Just a minute . . . I'll see.

    (The sound of the door closing is heard, and PANDORA *returns to the main room)*

Curt . . . Curt?

CURT *(Setting up his chess pieces; in a bored voice)*
Yeah, baby?

PANDORA
There's a guy named Art out here who says you told him to drop around.

CURT (*Not looking at her but down at the board*)
Invite him in, baby.

(*PANDORA exits*)

RICH
Is this the guy?

CURT (*Nods, in low voice*)
Never a dull moment . . . right, Rich?

RICH (*Sarcastic*)
Yeah. We're really in ta somethin', man.

> (*The music changes during the remainder of this scene. "Delilah" and "Parisian Thoroughfare" as recorded by Max Roach and Clifford Brown play. These will be the theme for the scenes between ART and PANDORA, except when other music is necessary to stress altering moods. If Act I extends long enough, "Sketches in Spain" by Miles Davis is to be played also, but "Delilah" should be replayed during PANDORA's box scene*)

PANDORA (*Offstage*)
Just a minute.

> (*. . . and the noise of the lock and chain is followed by ART's . . .*)

ART
Good evening.

> (*She leads him into the living room.*)
>
> RICH *has poured beer for* CURT *and himself; he stands and saunters to the radio as if to change stations, but turns after* ART *has passed behind him and sizes up the stranger from the rear*)

CURT *(Stands)*
Hey, good buddy! You found the place okay, huh?

ART *(Pleased by greeting)*
Yeah, it wasn't so hard to find but I guess I came around to the wrong door.

CURT *(With a wave)*
Awww . . . that's okay. One's good as the other. It's better to come in that way if you're walkin' from Washington Boulevard. You live somewhere 'round there, don't ya?

ART *(Hesitant)*
Well . . . I did.

CURT *(Gesturing)*
Here, I want you to meet my wife and a buddy of mine.
    (Introducing PANDORA*)*
This is my wife, Pandora . . . and . . .

PANDORA *(Smiles brightly)*
We already met, kinda. He told me his name at the door.

CURT *(Ignoring* PANDORA*)*
. . . and this is Rich.

RICH *(Remains in same spot.* ART *turns and* RICH *gives him a casual salute)*
What's happen'n, brother?

CURT *(To* PANDORA *and* RICH*)*
This is a guy I met in jail.
    (Introduces ART*)*
Art Garrison.
    (Shows ART *a seat on the couch, downstage from* RICH*)*
Yeah, Art was one of the best young cons on Tier Three . . .
    (To PANDORA*)*
Get my boy here a drink, baby.

PANDORA *(Starts for kitchen)*
You drink beer, Art?

ART
Sure . . . that sounds great.

PANDORA *(Over her shoulder)*
We got some scotch, if you want it.

ART
No, thanks.

> (RICH *sits, makes opening move, not looking at* ART)

CURT *(To* RICH)
Yeah, if it wasn't for Art here I wouldn't be sittin' here.

RICH *(Bored)*
Yeah?

CURT
This is the kid who banged Scooter aside the jaw during the riot last summer in the joint.

RICH *(Sounding more enthused)*
Yeah . . . you were doin' a stretch down at county jail when that happened, weren't you?

CURT
Yeah, man. I was there bigger den shit.
> *(Takes seat. During the telling of the incident,* PANDORA *stands framed in the kitchen doorway, watching the men)*

Yeah, that paddy mathafukker, Scooter, was comin' down on me with an icepick, man . . . we had all been rumblin' up and down the cell block and I slipped on somethin' wet . . . I think it was Cory's blood 'cause Miles and his boys had stomped the mathafukker so good . . . And I went to look up and all I could see was that grey-eyed mathafukkin' Scooter comin' at me with that icepick of his . . . He reached down and

grabbed my shirt front and drew back his arm and *whammo* . . .
> (*Indicating* ART)

. . . just like a bat outa hell my boy here had scored on the sucker's jaw.

ART *(Pleased)*
Well . . . I couldn't let that white sonna bitch do you in, man.

RICH *(Dryly)*
What was the beef about, man?

CURT
Well, you know Miles goes for the Muslims though he ain't one hisself. Now the Muslims were in a hassle at the joint with the guards and the big people up top because of their religious beliefs, dig?

RICH *(Interested)*
What do you mean?

CURT
Well, the guards didn't want them havin' their meetin's 'cause they said they were organizin' and plottin'. And the Muslims wanted some of the chow changed 'cause they don't eat the same kinda food that we do.

RICH
Yeah!

CURT
So while this was all goin' on, Cory . . . a young, wise nigger who thinks he's inta somethin' . . . well he started agitatin' and signifyin' 'bout who the Muslims think they was. And what made it so rank was a lot of the ofays start in sayin' things they had held back before, so Miles and some of the boys got together one day and caught that little jive sucker Cory outside his cell block and stomped him so bad the deck was greasy wit' his blood, man. That's when the shit started really goin'

down, right there, man. Bumpy, Cory's cousin, come runnin' up, man, and that big nigger kicked Miles square in the nuts and laid out two of his boys before the rest of them got themselves together. By that time some of the whiteys come runnin' up and a few more of Miles' boys. Yeah, the whole shit started right there where Cory lay almost done in . . .

RICH
Yeah . . . I heard a couple of cats got stabbed, man.

CURT
Yeah, man, it was pretty scary for a while, mostly black cons against white ones except for the studs who just tried to stay out of the shit and the Uncle Toms . . . those Toms we were really out to cool.

RICH *(Heated)*
Yeah, you should have done those mathafukkers in!

CURT
Even the guards wouldn't come into the cell block and break it up at first . . . a whole lot of shit went down that day.
    (Looking at ART)
I owe my boy here a lot for that day.

ART *(Embarrassed)*
Yeah, man, I would have liked to have stayed out of it but I couldn't.

CURT
Yeah, Art, I us'ta wonder about that . . .
    (A two-beat pause)
. . . How could you just go about your business and stay in the middle all the time in that place when so much crap was goin' down?

ART
I just stayed out of everything, that's all.

CURT
But didn't you care about anything, man? Didn't you feel anything when that shit was happen'n to you?

ART
Yeah, I cared but I just didn't let it bother me too much. I just froze up on everything that tried to git in and not too much touched me.

PANDORA *(From doorway)*
Talk about somebody bein' cold!

CURT *(Having noticed her in doorway for first time, stares at ART)*
But you don't know how I appreciate what you did, man. It wasn't your fight, man. You weren't takin' sides. You were one of the quiet guys waitin' for trial who just kept his mouth shut and minded his own business.

ART
I never do try and take sides in stir, just serve my time and forget about it, that's all.

> (PANDORA *moves out of the doorway into the kitchen)*

CURT
Well, I'm glad you did that time, man, and if there's anything I can ever . . .

> (RICH *interrupts)*

RICH
What were you in for, Art?

> (CURT *takes a drink of his beer, lights a ciga-rette and blows smoke across the table above the two men's heads.* PANDORA *drops something made of glass in the kitchen and curses)*

ART
Well . . . I was waiting for trial . . . attempted murder.

RICH
That's a tough one to have on your rap sheet.

ART
Yeah, it doesn't do your record or you any good, especially when it ain't for money.

CURT *(Finally makes answering chess move)*
It was over a broad, wasn't it?

ART *(Lights a cigarette, offers* RICH *a light but is refused)*
Yeah. I guess girls are my main weakness.

RICH *(With unlit cigarette dangling from his lips, makes move)*
How much time did you do?

ART
Waited on my trial for nine months at county when the husband of the girl dropped the charges and left town.

CURT *(Replies to move)*
That's who you shot, the girl's husband?

ART *(His eyes following game)*
Yeah.

RICH *(Moves quickly)*
You pretty good with a gun?

ART *(Caught up in game)*
I can usually hold one without it blowing my foot off.

RICH *(Sharply)*
Any simple ass can do that! I asked you are you any good with one!

> *(The three men are fixed in tableau for a three-beat interval;* ART *strains forward from his seat and is about to speak)*

CURT *(To* RICH *as he makes his move)*
This move's goin' ta show ya ta stop fuckin' with Curt the Kid, good buddy.

> *(Noise of refrigerator door opening and slamming, and* PANDORA *enters with a bottle and a glass. She pours beer for* ART *and sets the glass down beside him as the men all look at the chessboard)*

PANDORA *(In a light mood)*
Sorry I took so long, Art. I just dropped the supper.
   (To CURT)
Honey, the beans are all messed up. Little Mamma
won't have anything to eat 'cept eggs.

CURT *(Not looking at her)*
Didn't want no fuckin' beans anyhow! And I know
Mamma Too Tight don't want any either . . . what
kinda shit is that . . . givin' that broad beans on her
first night on the streets?

PANDORA *(Defensively)*
That's all we got, honey . . . You know we won't have
any spendin' money until Deeny pays me.

RICH
Why don't you have a seat, Pan?

PANDORA
I gotta finish cleanin' the kitchen . . . I don't want no
roaches 'round here. Last place we had we had to split
'cause the roaches took it over. The little mathafukkers
got mo' of the food than Curt or me. Soon as I bring
in a little money to get some food with . . .

   (CURT *looks at her sharply but she is turned
   toward* RICH *and* ART)

. . . there's mo' of them little mathafukkers there than
your eyes could see. And I put too much time in fixin'
this pad up nice the way it is to have them little
mathafukkers move in on me and try to take it over.

CURT
You better finish up, sweetcake, so I can take you to
work.
   *(The term "sweetcake" is used with derision,
   seldom with affection, in this play.*

   PANDORA *picks up* CURT's *empty bottles and
   exits)*

Your move, Richie.

RICH
Are you sure, man?

CURT
Just ask Art, he's been watchin' the game.

ART
Well, I ain't in it, man.

RICH
That's right, you ain't in it.

CURT *(Watching ART's face)*
Yeah, it's your move, Richie, babe.

RICH *(To ART)*
That was pretty nice of that girl's ole man to let you off, Art.

ART
Nawh . . . he wanted his ole lady to leave the state with him so he had to drop the charges against me to let her off the hook too.

RICH
She was in it too, huh?

ART
She shot him with me.

CURT
You play this game, Art?

ART
Yeah, some. But I haven't had much practice lately.

CURT
Well, this one's about over.

RICH *(Snorts)*
Sheeet!

CURT
Maybe you'd like ta play the winner.

RICH *(Grimacing before making hesitant move)*
Where ya livin' now, Art?

ART
I just got locked out of my room.

RICH
Yeah, Curt said you wanted to make some money.

ART *(Intensely)*
I have to, man. I'm really on my ass.

CURT
Check!

RICH *(Makes move)*
Not yet, sucker.

ART
I gotta get out of this town.

RICH
You got a car, ain't ya?

CURT *(Moves)*
Not long now, Rich.

ART
Yeah, that's about all I got. A car and a suitcase. I've also gotten more jail time in this town than in my whole life, and I've been halfway 'round the world and all over this country.

RICH *(Moves and acts angry)*
Yeah, L.A.'s no fuckin' good, man. If I was off parole now I would get the first thing on wheels out of here. How 'bout you, Curt? If you weren't out on bail wouldn't you make it?

> (CURT *doesn't answer.*
>
> *Stage left, a knock sounds, and* PANDORA *comes out of the kitchen striding toward the entrance which serves as the front door to the apartment)*

PANDORA
That must be Little Mamma.

CURT
Sure hope it is . . . I would really like ta see that little broad.

PANDORA *(Peers through window)*
Yeah, there's that chick.
 (Calling outside in jocular way)
Hey, broad, what they doin' lettin' you outta jail?

 (An indistinct shout and a laugh come from outside)

CURT *(To* RICH)
Checkmate, man!

 (Lights lower to blacken the stage)

ACT I

SCENE 2

When the lights go up MAMMA TOO TIGHT and SHAKY sit upon the lowered bed. Faintly reflecting a glow, the bedspread gives them the appearance of sitting upon smoldering coals. MAMMA TOO TIGHT, a small, voluptuous girl, is dressed well. Her shift complements her creamy complexion and full-blown build. SHAKY is nondescript but dresses in expensive casual clothes.

CURT, RICH and ART sit in the same area, stage right, facing the bed, forming the lower lip of a half-moon, and PANDORA has changed to a black cocktail dress and sits upon the stairs to the bathroom. She faces front with a bit of red-ruffled slip peeking beneath and around her black-stockinged legs.

They all eat chicken from cardboard containers and reach for beers and cigarettes. The light in the kitchen is off, and the radio plays.

ART
Thanks again, Curt . . . if you hadn't invited me to eat I don't know what I'd do . . . probably had to drive downtown on what little gas I got and eat at one of those Rescue Missions.

MAMMA TOO TIGHT *(Nudging* SHAKY *in the ribs)*
Well, I'll be damned . . . Ole Curt done saved himself a soul.

SHAKY *(Slow and languid)*
Easy, baby, you gonna make me spill my beer.

MAMMA TOO TIGHT
What you know 'bout eatin' at Rescue Missions, boy?

PANDORA *(Interjecting)*
You better stop callin' that guy ah boy, Mamma . . .
ha ha . . . girl . . . you got mo' gall.

RICH *(Drinking beer)*
Yeah, Mamma, how fuckin' big do boys grow where
you come from?

RICH *(With food in mouth)*
Forget about it, Art, glad to have ya. One more don't
mean a thing.

PANDORA
Listen ta that, Mamma Too Tight . . .
    (Mocking)
. . . "One mo' mouf don't mean a thing." . . . We eat
beans all week and when you and Curt's friends come
in we play big shit! . . . And call out for food and beer.

> (CURT, SHAKY *and* ART *stop eating.* CURT
> *stares at* PANDORA, *and* ART *holds his plate
> like it is hot and he is trying not to drop it on
> the floor.* SHAKY *eyes* MAMMA TOO TIGHT
> *and gives a mean scowl.* MAMMA *has seen the
> look on* CURT's *face before.* RICH *goes on en-
> joying his meal)*

MAMMA *(In a jolly tone, to* PANDORA)
Girl, you don't have ta tell me a thing . . . these here
men think that money can be just picked up off'a them
pavements out there like chewin' gum paper . . . until
they got ta get out there for themselves.
    *(She swings off the bed and shows flashes of
    lingerie)*
Like this pretty boy here with the fuzz on his face.
    (She approaches ART *and stands so her hips*

form a prominent profile to CURT's *line of vision)*

He ain't even eatin' no mo' . . . and Curt's not either, honey. What I tell ya? These men are somethin' else. So weak from plottin' what we should be doin' to bring some money in that they can't eat themselves.

(Puts her plate on coffee table)

I know that Curt is a big strong man . . . he's always lettin' Pan know.

(Strong dialect)

. . . So he don't need no help from us frail-ass women but maybe ole fuzzy wuzzy face here needs some help.

(Her audience is in better humor once more.

To ART)

You wants Mamma Too Tight to feeds him some food, baby boy?

SHAKY
Cut out the Magnolia act. Everything wears thin, *Queenie!*

MAMMA *(Sudden anger)*
Don't you call me no fuckin' Queenie!

SHAKY *(Sarcastic)*
Anything you say, baby.

(PANDORA *guffaws at* SHAKY's *tone)*

PANDORA *(Mimicking* MAMMA's *drawl)*
But ain't dat yo name, hoon e e e ?

(MAMMA *ignores* SHAKY *and* PANDORA, *picks drumstick from plate and offers it to* ART, *who frowns, and she pulls it away and puts it to her mouth imitating a mother feeding a reluctant child. Finally,* ART *smiles at her as* SHAKY *speaks)*

SHAKY
Why don'chou lighten up, woman!

MAMMA
Lighten up? . . . Damn . . . man . . . I ain't here ten
minutes befo' I see your face and you tell *me* to lighten
up! I been with you since I hit the streets at noon
and you still checkin' up on me . . . Don't worry, man
. . . I'm goin' ta get right ta work.

SHAKY *(Slow and languid)*
I know that, baby.

MAMMA *(To PANDORA)*
Girl, you should of seen Shaky . . . ha ha ha . . . almost
swept me off my feet, girl. Said he loved me and
really missed me so much the last ninety days that he
almost went out of his mind . . . ha ha . . .
   (Coyly)
I was so embarrassed and impressed, girl, I liked to
have blushed and nearly peed on myself like a sixteen-
year-old girl.
   (Change of voice)
But the ole sonna bitch didn't fool me none with that
shit! . . . The only thing he missed was that good
steady money!

CURT *(Piqued)*
Why don't you check yourself, Mamma!

MAMMA *(Waving CURT's threat off and returning to
      the edge of the bed)*
But, girl, he sho' threw some lovin' on me . . . he heee
. . . sheeet, I should go away again after this afternoon.

      (PANDORA laughs throughout)

Ummm . . . chile . . . I nearly thought I was on that
honeymoon I never had.

PANDORA
You should after that routine, baby.

MAMMA
And then when the sun start goin' down and things

got really gettin' romantic, girl . . . this mathafukker
says . . .

> *(Lights lower; spot on bed.*

> SHAKY *speaks the line)*

SHAKY
I want you to bring in a yard tonight, baby.

> (MAMMA *resumes speech.*

> *Bed spot off; colored spot on* MAMMA)

MAMMA
You what, man?

> *(Colored spot off; bed spot on)*

SHAKY
A hundred stone cold dollars, baby. Tonight, baby!

> *(Spot off; lights go up)*

MAMMA *(To* PANDORA)
And girl, do you know what I said?

PANDORA
Yeah, I know what you said.

MAMMA
That's right, baby, I said to Shaky, "How do you want
them, daddy . . . in fives or tens?"

> *(Laughter halts the speeches and the glasses are
> filled and fingers cleaned of chicken grease and
> cigarettes are lit)*

CURT *(To* SHAKY)
Don't let Mamma try and fool you . . . she wanted to
see you so bad . . . every time Pan us'ta go visit her she
would say to Pan, "How's that ole dirty Shaky doin'?"

MAMMA
Yeah, I'd ask . . . 'cause I'd be wonderin' why ain't
the mathafukker down here.

SHAKY
Now, let's not go into that again, baby.

CURT
Yeah, Mamma . . . you know what's happen'n behind
that. You know why Shaky didn't come down . . . you
never can tell when they might have a warrant out
on him or somethin' and keep him too. You remember what happened at court, don't cha?

MAMMA
Yeah, I remember. How can I forget? The judge said
for Shaky to leave the court 'cause every time I'm on
trial he's in the back row hangin' 'round and that last
ole woman judge said she knew who Shaky was an'
she'd like to put him behind bars instead of me . . .
but comin' down to visit me in jail is different, Curt!

SHAKY (Pleading)
Now, baby . . .

CURT
Listen, Mamma . . . how old are you?

MAMMA
Twenty.

CURT
That means you're a big girl now, a woman who should
be able to understand things, right?

MAMMA
Yeah, but . . .

CURT (Cutting)
Right! Now listen, baby . . . and listen hard . . . now
how many times you been busted?

MAMMA
Thirty-three times . . . but I only fell this once for
more than ten days and that was because I got that
new fuckin' woman judge. I got the best record in
town of any broad on the block I know. Pandora's rap

sheet is worst than mine and I was on the block two years before she was.

CURT
Exactly, baby. Now if you didn't have an old man like Shaky out there workin' for you, you'd be out of business and servin' some big time . . . right? Wouldn't that be a drag to be servin' some grand theft time behind givin' up a little body!

Pan ain't been snatched since before we were married . . . ain't that right, Pandora? See there? Now let me tell you, baby, and listen hard.
    (Intensely)
A self-respectin' man won't let his ole lady stay in jail. If he can't get the bail for her or the juice to pay off somebody downtown like Shaky done you to have your time cut to one third . . .
    (Disgust)
. . . he's a punk! And any broad that even looks at the jive sucker should get her funky ass run into the ground like a piece of scum!

MAMMA *(On defensive)*
I know all that, Curt, but I got so lonely down there. Nothin' down there but broads and most of them butches.

PANDORA
Mamma . . . don't even talk about it. Makes cold chills run up my back just thinkin' 'bout it.

CURT
Yeah, we know it was hard, baby, but you can't afford to lose your old man by his gettin' busted behind a jail visit. That would be a stone trick, Mamma. Nothin' but a hummer . . . Right?

MAMMA
Awww . . . Curt, you try and make it sound so smooth.

PANDORA
He can really make it do that, girl.

RICH *(Finishes drinking the last of his beer)*
Hey, Shaky, I want you to take a walk with me, okay?

SHAKY *(Standing slowly and visibly rocking)*
Yeah, man.
> *(To* MAMMA*)*
I'll see you back at the house, baby. Watch yourself.

MAMMA
I'll probably be in early, Shaky. Unless I catch somethin' good.

> (RICH *and* SHAKY *exit by the front door.*
> PANDORA *accompanies them and checks the*
> *outside before they step out)*

Sheeet, Pandora, I thought Shaky was the Chicken Delight man when he knocked. I wasn't here ten minutes before he was knockin' on the door to see if I had my ride to the club. Didn't even think about feedin' me.
> *(Soulful)*
Just give me some good lovin' ta show me where it's at.

PANDORA
These men are somethin' else, girl . . . 'spect a girl to go outta here on an empty stomach and turn all kinds of tricks . . . but Curt and me did have some beans for you, girl, but I dropped them.

MAMMA
Well, I'm glad you did.

CURT *(Packing away chessboard)*
I told her you didn't want no beans, Mamma.

MAMMA
I got too many beans in the joint.

PANDORA *(Peeved)*
Well, that's what I had for you, chick.

MAMMA *(To* ART*)*
Hey, pretty baby, why you so quiet?

ART
Oh, I ain't got much to say, I guess.

CURT
This is my boy Art, Mamma. I introduced you when you came in.

MAMMA *(Sultry)*
I know his name . . . ha ha . . . I just want to know his game, dat's all. Hey, fuzz face, what's yo' game? Is you kinda fuzzy wuzzy 'round the edges?

ART
I'm sorry . . . I don't know . . .

CURT
Awww . . . he's okay, Mamma . . . he was in the joint with me. He's just quiet, that's all. Reads too much . . . somethin' you should do more of.

PANDORA
Why should she? Ain't heard of nobody gettin' no money readin'.

MAMMA *(To ART)*
Now I know your name, fuzzy boy, now you say my name.

ART *(Surprised)*
Your name?

MAMMA
Yeah. Say Ma-Ma Too Tight!

ART
I know your name.

MAMMA
But I want you to say it.

ART
I don't have to with you broadcasting it all over the place ever since you been here.

MAMMA *(Cross)*
You must think you're wise, man.

ART *(In low, even voice)*
I am, you big-mouthed bitch, and I want you to stop
jivin' with me.

> (PANDORA *giggles.* CURT *looks on enjoying
> the surprise showing on* MAMMA's *face)*

MAMMA
Well . . . 'scuse me, tiger.
> *(Walks over to* ART *and sits beside him)*
Awww . . . forget it. I always act this way, ask Pan
and Curt. 'Specially when I'm ah little bit loaded . . .
Hey, Pandora, your friend here ain't got no sense of
humor.

PANDORA
Nawh . . . he's too much like Curt. Serious. That's why
they probably get along so good, girl . . . they probably made for each other.

> *(The girls laugh)*

CURT
C'mon, Pan . . . it's almost time for you to go to work.
Deeny will be callin' nex' thing and that's one mathafukker I don't even want to see, much less talk to. Go
and get the stuff.

> (PANDORA *exits through the bathroom door)*

MAMMA *(To* ART*)*
You want to know why they call me Mamma Too
Tight, pretty baby?

CURT
If Shaky ever heard you callin' my boy that he'd break
your arm, Mamma.

MAMMA
Yeah, he might. But Shaky ain't where nothin's shakin'
at the moment. . . . Just out givin' Rich a fix . . .

CURT
Both of you bitches talk too much!

MAMMA *(To* ART)
You know what, fuzz wuzz? I sho' wish I had a li'l
fuzzy wuzzy like you up there some of those cold
nights in the joint.
> *(She gets up and walks to stand before the men.
> She plays it strictly for laughs, swinging her
> hips to the radio music, and singsongs in a
> hearty, brazen voice like one of the old-time red
> hot mammas.*

> *Singing)*

Why do they call me what they call me, baby? When
what they call me is my name.

ART *(Dryly)*
I have suspicions but I'm not positive.

MAMMA *(Ridiculing, but friendly)*
You have suspicions as every little fuzzy wuzzy does
but let me tell you . . . because my real name is
Queenie Mack! Queenie Bell Mack! Ain't that some
shit? No self-respectin' whore in the world can go
'round with a name like that unless she's in Mississippi . . . sheeet . . . *Queenie!*

ART
So you named yourself Mamma Too . . .

MAMMA *(Cutting)*
No! It just happened. I don't know how. I just woke
up one day with my name that way . . . And I like
it that way . . . it's me!
> *(Turning toward* ART)
Don't you think it fits, honey?

ART
I think it really does.

MAMMA
Damn right it does. It makes me feel so alive. That's
why I'm glad to be out . . .

CURT *(Yelling)*
Hey, Pandora!

MAMMA
Man, but it's so good to be high again. It's so good
to be free.

> (PANDORA *enters from the bathroom and de-
> scends the stairs and places a cardboard box on
> the table as the lights blacken briefly and the
> music rises)*

ACT I

SCENE 3

As the lights go up and the music lowers, the scene has shifted. CURT and PAN-DORA sit upon the couch, across from ART, and MAMMA TOO TIGHT has taken the stool CURT was seated on. Un-covered, the box waits in the center of the table. CURT is licking a brown cigarette as the theme plays.

CURT
Yeah. We want to make some money, Art, so we can get out of this hole.
> (Lights the cigarette and inhales fiercely. Drops head. Two-beat pause. In strained voice, holding smoke back)
We're makin' it to Buffalo, man. You hip to Buffalo?

ART
No, I don't think so . . .

CURT (Takes another drag)
It's a good little hustlin' town, I hear. I got a case comin' up here for passin' some bad paper, ya know, forgin' payroll checks . . . and when I get the money to make restitution and give the people downtown some juice, ya know, man, pay them off, I'm makin' it East. But I need some grand theft dough.

ART
But won't you get some time with your record?

CURT
Nawh. Probably not. You see, I'm a good thief. I make money by my wits . . . ya know, with a pen or by talkin'

some sucker out of it. It's only seldom that I'm forced to really take any money by force.

If I make full restitution for these checks and fix my lawyer up and the other people downtown, I'll get probation. They'll reduce it to a misdemeanor, and breakin' probation for somethin' like that ain't nothin' . . . besides, Buffalo's a long way away, man.

PANDORA *(Receiving cigarette from* CURT)
It's supposed to be a good little town. A different scene entirely. I'm due for a good scene for a change.

CURT
Yeah, but we have to get that juice money first, baby. We gotta get us some long money.

MAMMA
Any place is better than L.A. but I heard that Buffalo is really boss.

PANDORA *(Languid)*
It sho' is, baby.

MAMMA
I wonder if I could get Shaky to go?

CURT
Sure you could, Mamma. He can get connections to deal his stuff there just like here. That's the idea. When we make our hit and split out of here we're goin'a take as many as we can with us. You know, set up a kinda organization.

PANDORA *(Passing cigarette to* MAMMA)
They really got respect for cats from the coast back there.

ART *(Getting caught up in the mood)*
Yeah, they really do . . . when I . . .

PANDORA *(Cutting speech)*
With me workin' on the side and with Curt dealin' we'd be on our feet in no time.

CURT
We want to be on our feet when we get there, baby.

ART
And that's where I come in, right?

CURT
Right, good buddy.

MAMMA *(Handing cigarette to* ART*)*
Here, baby.

ART *(Waving it away)*
So what's on your mind, Curt?

MAMMA *(Extending cigarette)*
I said here, baby, I just don't like to hold this thing and see all this bread go up in ashes.

ART
I don't want any.

> *(A three-beat stop, all caught in tableau staring at* ART*; then* PANDORA *snickers and breaks into a tittering laugh, looking at* CURT*)*

PANDORA *(Ridicule)*
You and your friends, Curt ... I thought ...

CURT *(Heated)*
Shut up, bitch ... you talk too much!

PANDORA *(Rising anger)*
Why shouldn't I when you bring some square-ass little ...

> (CURT *slaps her; she jumps to her feet and spins to claw him but* CURT *lunges forward and slaps her again, causing her to trip backward across the edge of the coffee table.*
>
> *From the floor, removing one of her shoes)*

Goddamn you, Curt ...
> *(She begins to crawl to her knees and* CURT *moves around the table after her. Then* ART

steps between them and pushes CURT *backward on the couch. Surprise is upon* CURT's *face and* MAMMA TOO TIGHT *seems frozen in place)*

CURT
What the fuck's goin' on, man?

ART *(Low)*
Don't hit her any more, Curt.

CURT *(Incredulous)*
What? . . . Man, are you payin' this woman's bills . . . have you got any papers on her?

PANDORA *(To* CURT)
Are you payin' my bills, mathafukker?

CURT *(Rising to attack* PANDORA; ART *blocks his way)*
I've told you to keep your mouth . . .
　　　(To ART *when he won't let him pass)*
Now listen, Art, you're like a brother to me but you don't know what's goin' down, man.

ART
Why don't we all sit down and try to relax, Curt? Why don't you do it for me, huh? As a favor. I'm sorry for buttin' in to your business between you and your old lady but somethin' just happens to me, man, when I see a guy hit a girl.

　　　(After a minute, CURT *is soothed and sits upon the couch again, glaring at* PANDORA, *who holds her shoe like a weapon)*

MAMMA *(Partially recovered)*
Oh, man, I just hit the streets and this is what I run into . . .

CURT *(Intense, to* ART)
What are you doin', man? Squarin' out on me? Man, I've went a long way . . .

ART *(Leaning forward)*
Well, look, Curt . . . I can split . . .

(CURT *stands and looks down on* ART. *Changing expression,* PANDORA *makes a move for the box but* CURT *waves her hand away)*

CURT

No, I don't think you better try that, Art.
　　(Pause)
Tell me, Art. Why don't you want to smoke any marijuana?

ART

Why don't . . . I don't understand why you should ask me that.

CURT

Is your playin' hero for Pandora a game to cover up somethin', man?

　　(MAMMA *is clutching herself as if she has returned to the womb)*

MAMMA

Oh . . . shit shit shit . . . shit . . . just today . . . just today they cut me loose . . . just today.

PANDORA *(No longer angry, placing hand on* CURT's *arm)*

Easy, baby, I think he's okay.

CURT

You would!

ART

Now, look, man, I don't put down anybody for doin' what they want but just don't hassle me!

PANDORA *(Hostile, to* ART)

Cool it, baby, you're in some deep trouble now.

MAMMA

Oh, Goddamn . . . why can't I just be plain-ass Queenie Bell Mack?

CURT *(Low)*

What's happen'n, brother?

ART
I just don't get high . . . that's all . . .

MAMMA *(Nearly screaming)*
Neither does J. Edgar Hoover, sucker, but he don't
come in here pretend'n to be no friend!

PANDORA *(Enraged, fearful of losing control, to*
        MAMMA)
*Shut up, bitch! This is Curt and our place. We got
mo' to lose than just our ass. Just shut on up!*

> (MAMMA *looks most like a small girl with
> wide, moist eyes)*

CURT
For the last time, Art, tell me somethin'.

ART
I just don't . . .

> (PANDORA *stands and moves in front of*
> CURT. *The coffee table separates them from*
> ART, *but she leans over)*

PANDORA *(To* CURT, *behind her)*
He's alright, honey. If he were a cop he'd be smokin'
stuff right along with us . . . you know that . . .

ART *(Bewildered)*
A cop! . . .

PANDORA *(Sarcastic)*
He's just a little square around the edges, Curt . . .

> *(Silence, then:*

> *To* ART)
But why, honey?

ART *(Shrugging sheepishly)*
I had a bad experience once behind pot, that's all.

> (MAMMA *chuckles until* CURT *stops her)*

MAMMA
He had a bad experience . . . hee hee hee . . . ha ha ha . . .
He had . . .

CURT *(Menace)*
Pan has already told you to check yourself, woman,
he's still my friend.

PANDORA
What was it all about, man . . . can you tell us about it?

ART
I'd rather not . . .

CURT *(Cutting)*
We know you'd rather not but . . .

PANDORA *(Cutting)*
Now look, Art, you're not givin' us much of a break
. . . we don't want to act like this but we got a lot of
the future riding on what happens in the nex' few
days. Why don't you tell us?

ART
I would but it don't seem that much . . .

CURT *(Not so threatening)*
But it is, Art!

PANDORA
C'mon, trust me. Can't you say anything? We've gone
more than half . . .

CURT
Stop rankin' him, will ya!

PANDORA
I'm only doin' it for you!

>   *(Silence as CURT and PANDORA stare at each
>   other)*

ART
Yeah, I'll talk about it . . .

(CURT *sits.* PANDORA *moves around the table closer to* ART. *The cigarette has been dropped by* MAMMA *beside the box.* "Delilah" *plays*)

You see . . . it was about three years ago. I shipped out on a freighter . . . ya know, one of those scows that fly the Panamanian or Liberian flag but don't really belong to any country . . .

MAMMA *(In small girl's voice)*
Ain't they American?

ART
Well, in a way. They belong to American corporations and the businessmen don't want to pay high taxes on 'em. They're pretty ratty.

(PANDORA *makes a seat on the floor between the men*)

Well, I went on a four-month cruise, ya know, to ports around the West Indies and then to North Africa.

MAMMA
Wow . . . that sounds gassy . . . I wish . . .

PANDORA *(Cutting)*
Mamma!

ART
Well, I been blowin' weed since I was about twelve . . .

MAMMA *(Ridicule)*
Ha ha ha . . . since he was twelve . . .

(PANDORA *and* CURT *frown at her and she huddles in her seat and looks cold*)

ART
. . . and everything was cool. I smoked it when I ran into it and never thought about it much unless someone turned me on. But in Tangier it was about as easy to get as a bottle of beer. Man, I had a ball all the

while I was over there and before I left I bought a big bag.

(Showing with his hands)

This big for about five bucks. All the way back on my night watches I just smoked grass and just thought of what the guys on my corner back home would say when I would pull out a joint or two and just give it to them. Prices back East are about triple what they are here, so you can guess what it was worth . . . And all the broads I would make . . . you know how it goes . . . take a broad up to your room and smoke a little weed and if you have anything goin' for you at all, man, that's it.

PANDORA *(Disgust)*

Yeah, there's a lot of stupid broads in this world.

ART *(Sensing the reduced tension)*

And I could still sell some when my money got low and come out beautiful. I was really feeling good about that grass, Curt.

Well, this tub docks in Philly about one A.M. and I have to leave ship and when I get to the station I find that my train don't leave until two the next afternoon. I got my pay and my belongings, so I stash most of my bags in a locker at the station, the bag of weed is in one but I have about half a dozen joints on me. Now I know Philly a little. I know where there's an after-hours joint so I grab a cab and go over there. The place is jumpin' . . . they're havin' a fish fry, and I start in drinkin' and talkin' to girls but none of them are listen'n 'cept for seven bucks for them and three for the management for rentin' one of the upstairs rooms, and I ain't buyin no cock . . . not in the States . . .

PANDORA

Well, I'm glad of that. I can take squares but not tricks, baby.

CURT *(To* PANDORA)
You still runnin' your mouth, ain't you?

ART
So I start talkin' with some guy and he tells me of a place he knows 'cross town that's better than this one. He looks okay to me. A blood. Dressed real sharp with a little goatee and everything. I had been talkin' to him about bein' out to sea and since he don't try and con me into a crap game and is buyin' one drink for every one of mine, I don't give a damn where we go 'cause I got the whole night to kill.

MAMMA
Oh, wow . . . I know this is the bad part . . .

PANDORA
Listen, Mamma.

MAMMA *(Turning her face away)*
I don't like to hear bad things.

ART
So we drinkin' bottles of beer and drivin' up Broad Street in Philly in his old wreck of a Buick and I think how it would be nice to turn on and get really loaded before we get where we're goin'. So I reach for my pocket but it's wintertime and I got on a pea jacket and sweaters and I have trouble gettin' to my pocket. And while I was lookin' I start in laughin'.

CURT
Laughin'?

ART
Yeah. I start wonderin' what would happen if this was a cop I was with and the idea was just too much. So funny. So I started in laughin'. And the guy asks me what I was laughin' at and I said I was just laughin' about him bein' a cop. And he said that he was and how did I know.
        (Two-beat pause)

I don't know how I got out of that car or away from him. But soon after I was pukin' my guts up, and I threw those joints into a sewer and they wouldn't go down 'cause snow and ice was cloggin' it up. And I was stompin' on 'em so they would go down and gettin' sick and after a while my feet were all covered with ice and snow and puke and marijuana . . . Ya know . . . I had nearly twenty bucks worth of dope frozen to the soles of my shoes.

MAMMA *(Seriously)*
Awww . . . no, man . . . I can't stand any more.

PANDORA *(Giggling)*
That's the best trip I've been on this week, Art.

ART
Nawh, really . . . baby. And the bag . . . I left it in a locker. Not the one I used but another empty one.

MAMMA
Those janitors must'a naturally been happy the next day.

ART
Yeah, they must have been but I couldn't even think of the stuff for a long time without wanting to heave up my guts.

CURT
That must'a been pretty scary, man.

> (PANDORA *has reached over and gotten the cigarette and re-lit it)*

PANDORA *(Offering it to* ART)
Now it's time to get back on the horse, cowboy.

ART *(Placing hand on stomach)*
I don't think I can.

MAMMA
You'll never think about that time in Philly again after the first drag, baby.

CURT
C'mon, man, you're already one of us. Do you think I'd bring you in if I thought you'd be a square?

PANDORA
Don't say that, Curt. He's not. Somethin' like what happened to him can mess up your mind about things.
(*She stands over him and puffs on the cigarette.*

Staring at him)
Now don't think about anything . . . just look into my eyes.
(*She inhales once more and gives the cigarette to* ART)
Now, here, put it in your mouth.

ART (*Takes it and puts to lips*)
I can do it all right but I just don't want to.

PANDORA (*Staring*)
Look into my eyes and inhale. Don't think about it being in your hand.

(ART *inhales and looks at her*)

All the way down now and hold it.

MAMMA
Don't ever say you don't believe in witches, boy.

CURT
Cool it, Mamma!

PANDORA
Now one more drag, Art.

(ART *takes another puff and hands the reefer to* CURT. ART *has a great grin on his face*)

ART
So that's what's in Pandora's box?

(*Lights change*)

PANDORA (*Fantasy*)
Among other things, Art. Among other things. But

those have been lies you've been told about bad things comin' out of Pandora's box.

MAMMA
Most people think that a girl's box is in other places.

PANDORA
Nothin' can be found bad in there either. People only bring evil there with them. They only look for evil there. The sick . . .

ART
What do you mean by sick?

PANDORA
The come freaks, that's who. The queers who buy sex from a woman.

MAMMA *(Bitterly)*
Yeah, they say we're wrong but they're the queers . . . payin' for another person's body.

CURT *(In euphoria, musing)*
Art, my man, we're goin' a Buffalo . . . goin' on day real soon.

PANDORA *(Repulsion)*
Some of them are real nice-lookin' cats. Not old with fat greasy bellies. Real nice-lookin' studs.
        (Bitterly)
Those are the real queers you have ta watch. They want ta hurt women.

MAMMA
You hip ta that, baby? Those muscle cats, you know, muscle queens . . . always wantin' ta freak out on ya.

ART
And that's all that comes out of Pandora's box?

        (CURT *pulls a nickel-plated revolver out of the box*)

CURT
No. Right now this is the most important thing.

There's always something new in there.
    (*Handing gun to* ART)
Feel it, brother.

    (ART *takes the gun. He is caught up in the music and with his new friends*)

ART
It's a good one.

MAMMA
Look how it shines.

    (*Lights change*)

ART (*Dreamlike*)
Yeah . . . like Pandora's eyes.

    (*Lights change*)

PANDORA (*Fantasy*)
Nothin' bad comes out of me or from my box, baby. Nothin' bad. You can believe that. It's all in what you bring to us.

    (*Lights change*)

MAMMA
That's wha's happen'n baby.

CURT
It's yours now, Art, as much yours as mine. Can you handle it, brother?

ART (*Looking at* PANDORA *and taking a new reefer*)
If that's my job, brother.

    (*The cigarette has been replaced by a new one and others are in the hands of the group;* PANDORA *drags in deeply*)

PANDORA
Buffalo's goin'a be a gas.

    (*The phone rings from the dressing room and*

CURT *goes to answer. His shadow can be seen upon the wall at the top of the stairs)*

CURT *(Off)*
Yeah, Deeny . . . yeah yeah yeah . . . yeah, man . . . yeah.

MAMMA
Who ever heard of a telephone in the toilet?

PANDORA
It's in the dressing room next to the bathroom, Mamma.

MAMMA
Sho' is strange . . . Hey, are you goin' a Buffalo too, fuzz wuzz?

ART
It looks that way.

PANDORA *(Smiling)*
I think I'll like that, Art. I think that'll be nice.

(A knock sounds at the front door.

CURT's *shadow hangs up the phone and retreats further into the area)*

CURT *(Off)*
Pandora! Move! Goddamn it! Get a move on!

(ART *stands as* PANDORA *jumps to her feet. He has a cross expression as he looks toward the dressing room entrance)*

ART *(To* PANDORA)
Can I help you?

(PANDORA *shakes her head)*

Is there anything I can do?

PANDORA
No, I don't think anybody can do anything, especially you.

(She places the gun and the marijuana in the box and hurries up the stairs.

The knock comes again)

MAMMA *(Still seated, toward door)*
Just a minute!

    (ART *watches* PANDORA *enter dressing room)*

You want to get the door, Art?

ART
I learned once never to open another man's door.

    (PANDORA and CURT, in coats, come from the dressing room; PANDORA has her costumes in her arms.

    MAMMA TOO TIGHT *gets up and walks downstage)*

CURT
That fuckin' Deeny wants you to rehearse some new music before your act, Pan.

PANDORA
Sonna bitch! Always late payin' somebody and always wantin' you to work your ass off.

CURT
Is your car parked far, Art?

ART
Not too far.

MAMMA *(Looking out window)*
It's only Rich.

CURT
Good. He can stay here and watch the phone while we're at the club. First we'll stop and get you some gas, Art, and then you can take us to the Strip Club.

PANDORA
Is your car big enough to get us all to the Strip Club on Western, Art?

ART
It'll even get us as far as Buffalo, Pandora.

> *(They exit.* RICH *enters, turns in doorway and is seen talking to someone outside. Then he shuts door, saunters gracefully across the room and turns the radio off. Lights dim out as he sprawls upon the couch)*

CURTAIN

ACT II

The curtain opens showing the Strip Club, or, rather, the suggested representation of a cheap night club in the Wilshire area of Los Angeles, featuring "Bronze" strip-teasers. But the effect should be directed toward the illusions of time, place and matter. Reality is questionable here. The set should be painted in lavish phony hues except for the bare brown floor. Seeing the set, the female audience should respond, "gorgeous, lovely, marvelous, delightful," and similar banalities. The men should wonder if the habitat of whores is not indeed the same region as their creatures of private myth, dream and fantasy.

A rotating color-wheel, in front of the major lights, should turn constantly throughout this scene, giving an entire spectrum of altering colored shadows. Additional colored lights and spots should be used to stress mood changes and the violence of the ending scene.

A MUSICIAN plays randomly at the piano. He is tall, wearing a dark suit with an open-necked dark shirt. The BARTENDER, wiry with his head shaven clean, sweeps the floor and empties ashtrays. A few CUSTOMERS sit and watch the MUSICIAN, and later the group, as the show hasn't begun.

The voice which is heard at the close of this act can be that of a CUSTOMER.

Two other MUSICIANS enter and climb upon the stage.

PIANO PLAYER *(Joking, to* BASS PLAYER *seated at piano)*
Hey, man, they lookin' for bass players all up and down the street but you cats are all bangin' out chords on out-of-tune pianos.

BASS PLAYER
What's happin'n, man? Say . . . listen to this . . .
(He plays a couple of frames)
What about that, man . . . huh?

PIANO PLAYER
Man, like I said . . . you're a damn good bass man . . .

BASS PLAYER *(Getting up)*
What you say about somebody lookin' for bass men?
. . . Man! Turn me on. I wouldn't be here in this trap if I knew where one of those gigs were.

DRUMMER *(Seated, working up a beat)*
Yeah, man, they need you like they need me.

PIANO *(Wryly)*
How's it feel to keep gettin' replaced by a jukebox?

> (BASS PLAYER *begins working with* DRUM-MER. PIANO PLAYER *strikes a few chords, then lights a cigarette)*

BASS
Hey, where's Stew and Ronny? I want to practice those new charts before Pandora gets in.

PIANO *(Blowing smoke out)*
They quit.

BASS *(Halting)*
What!

DRUMMER
Deeny wouldn't pay them this afternoon and pushed the new charts on them. They didn't want to learn new scores, not getting paid the money owed them, so they quit.

BASS
Just like that . . . they quit?

PIANO
This is our last night here, too. Deeny's in trouble with the union. No more gigs here until the hearin'.

BASS
Awww, man . . . there's always some shit with that jive-ass sucker. Is we gettin' our bread from Deeny tonight?

DRUMMER
Who knows? He don't have to pay until the last performance, and the union says stay on the gig until tonight.

BASS
We always gettin' put in some cross . . .

PIANO
Yeah, man. But jukeboxes don't go on strike and Deeny knows we know it, so let's take care of business.

BASS
Man, don't tell me that . . . the broads can't dance to no jukebox.

PIANO (*Seriously*)
Why not, man?

BASS
It just ain't done, man. No machine ain't never goin' a take a musician's play from him when it comes to providin' music for shows.

PIANO
Don't believe it, baby . . . in a couple of mo' years they'll find a way. Broads will be shakin' their cans to canned music just as good as to your playin' or mine and the customers will be payin' even higher prices . . . Nobody wins, man. Least of all us. C'mon, let's hit it . . .

(He begins playing "Delilah" as PANDORA, MAMMA TOO TIGHT *and* CURT *make their entrance. The girls wave to the* MUSICIANS *and stop at the bar, then move to a table near the bandstand.* PANDORA *places her costumes on an empty chair of a nearby table.* CURT *stands with his back to the bar)*

Okay. That's better . . . c'mon . . . Cook! . . .

BASS *(Not enthused, to* MAMMA *who waves again)*
Hey, pretty girl . . .

    (ART walks in, saunters to the cigarette machine; CURT *joins the girls)*

CURT
Hey, I wonder where everybody's at?

DRUMMER *(Stopping, followed by others)*
Hey . . . hey . . . what's the use of this fuckin' shit? . . .

PIANO
What's happen'n now, man?

    (DRUMMER hops from stage)

MAMMA
Damn . . . Stew and Ronny must be late, Pan.

PANDORA *(To* BARTENDER*)*
What happened to your boss, Deeny, Chico?

    (BARTENDER ignores her)

DRUMMER *(To* PIANO PLAYER*)*
Not a thing, man . . . everything's cool . . .
    (Goes to bar, to BARTENDER*)*
Hey, Chico. Give me a screwdriver and charge it to your boss.

BARTENDER
Deeny ain't in the charity business, baby.

    (ART sits down with his friends. One of the CUSTOMERS *leaves)*

PANDORA *(To* BARTENDER)
Yeah, baby, give me the usual and give my friends what they want. Put it on my tab.

DRUMMER *(To* BARTENDER)
You let me and Deeny worry about that, cool breeze. Give me a screwdriver like I said.

> (BARTENDER *goes behind bar and begins mixing* DRUMMER'*s drink)*

BARTENDER *(Sullenly to* PANDORA)
When you gonna take care of that tab, sweetcake?

PANDORA *(Angry)*
When your fuckin' boss pays me, mister! Now get us our drinks, please!

CURT *(To* BASS PLAYER, *who stands beside in- strument)*
Where's Deeny?

> (PIANO PLAYER *has gotten off of stage and talks to* DRUMMER *at the bar. A* CUSTOMER *goes to jukebox and looks over the selections)*

PIANO
What's happen'n, man? We got to make this gig . . . that's what the union says.

DRUMMER
Fuck the union.

BASS *(To* CURT)
It's a mystery to me, Curt.

MAMMA *(To* BASS PLAYER)
That number's a gassy one, honey. Pan's gonna work by that, ain't she?

BASS
Looks that way, Mamma, if anybody works at all tonight.

PIANO *(To* DRUMMER)
Awww, man . . . you know I know how you feel . . .

DRUMMER
Well, just don't run that crap down to me. I'm just fed up. The union screws you out of your dues and the clubs fuck you every chance they get . . .

PIANO
It ain't exactly that way . . . now if . . .

MAMMA
Don't you like Pan's new number, Art?

> (ART *doesn't answer. The* CUSTOMER *drops a coin into the jukebox and punches a selection: "Something Cool" sung by June Christie is played*)

PANDORA *(To* ART *and* MAMMA)
Can't come in here one day without some shit goin' down. Where's the brass so I can rehearse?

MAMMA
They better get here soon, honey. It'll be too late after a while.

BASS *(To* PANDORA)
Forget about it, Pan. They ain't no brass tonight.
> *(To* PIANO PLAYER)

Well, I know all that, but it's no use rehearsin' without any brass and if this is our last night anyhow . . .

CURT *(Rising and going to the bar)*
You said this is the last night, man?

PANDORA *(To* BASS PLAYER)
No brass!

MAMMA *(To* ART)
You hear what he said?

BASS *(Putting down instrument)*
Hey, fix me a C.C. and ginger ale, Chico!

> (CUSTOMER *who played records goes to the bar and sits down*)

PANDORA *(To* BARTENDER)
Hey, what about our drinks, man!

BARTENDER
Okay, Pandora ... just a minute.

CURT
Hey, fellas ... what's goin' down?

> *(The* MUSICIANS *tell* CURT *about the trouble as the scene plays on in center stage at the table. The conversations should overlap as they have but become increasingly rapid and confusing if necessary.*
>
> *After the* MUSICIANS *are served the* BARTENDER *takes the orders at* PANDORA's *table as* CURT *continues to talk at the bar)*

PANDORA
Shit . . . no brass . . . musicians quittin' . . . I ain't got no job no more.

MAMMA
Yeah. It don't look so good, but perhaps Deeny can do somethin' when he comes in . . .

PANDORA
Deeny . . . shit . . . Deeny . . . all he can do! . . .
> *(Furious, searching for words)*
Why, shit, woman! Deeny can't even do numbers and shit cucumbers!

ART
Thanks for the drink, Pan.

PANDORA
Is that all you can do, man? Say thank you?

ART
No. It's not the only thing.

> (MAMMA *gets up and goes over to the* BASS PLAYER, *who drops out of the conversation between* CURT, *the other two* MUSICIANS *and the* BARTENDER.

GOIN' A BUFFALO

Another CUSTOMER *leaves, leaving only one sitting upon a stool, attempting to get the* BARTENDER's *attention)*

BARTENDER
Well look, man, I only work here. You better settle that with Deeny.

(Behind the bar the phone rings. The BARTENDER answers)

CURT
If that's Deeny I want to talk to him.

BARTENDER
Hey, man, I'm talkin' on the phone.

DRUMMER
Let me talk to the mathafukker!
(He tries to reach across the bar)

BARTENDER *(Backing off)*
Hey, cool it! Wait!

PIANO *(Grabbing DRUMMER's arm)*
Hold it, man!

DRUMMER
Take your fuckin' hands off me, baby!

BARTENDER
Wait, I said.

CURT
Tell Deeny I'm waitin' for him.

(DRUMMER breaks away from PIANO PLAYER and begins around the bar. BARTENDER reaches under bar for a weapon)

BARTENDER *(Shouts)*
Wait!!!

(The scene freezes in tableau except for the BARTENDER, PANDORA and CURT. Lights

go down to purples and deep shadow shades as an eerie spot plays upon the table. Occasionally from the shadows voices are heard.

In shadows)
Okay, Deeny. I'll be expectin' ya.

PANDORA *(To* ART*)*
So he's comin'.

ART
Yeah, no need to wait for very long now.

PANDORA
What else can you do, Art?

ART
What else can I do except say thank you, you mean?

PANDORA
Yeah. That's what I mean.

ART
I can wait, Pandora.

PANDORA *(Jolly)*
What's the good of waitin' when things have ta be done? Is that why you have to eat at Rescue Missions and get favors from friends, baby? 'Cause you waitin'? Tell me. What are you waitin' on, Art?

ART
Me? I'm just waitin' so I won't jump into somethin' too fast, and I think you should do the same.

PANDORA
I didn't know you gave out advice too. But I wish I could take some of it. Ya see, we're already in the middle of some deep shit . . . There just ain't time to sit back and cool it, honey . . .

ART *(Disregarding the ridicule in her voice, soothing)*
Yes, you can . . . just sit back and look around and wait a while. You don't have to do anything . . . baby, the whole world will come to you if you just sit back and be ready for it.

PANDORA *(Serious)*
I wish I could. But so much has to be done and we keep fallin' behind.

BARTENDER *(In shadows)*
Now what can I do, man? Deeny left with Pete and he said he'd be right back and for you guys to practice with the girls.

> *(One of the* CUSTOMERS *who walked out enters with a* SHOWGIRL. *She is dark and thin and pretty in a tinseled way. They stop in the shadows and whisper and the girl separates from him, enters the light, passes through and heads toward the dressing rooms in the rear. The* CUSTOMER *takes a seat at the bar. He is engulfed by shadows and becomes frozen in place like the others)*

PANDORA *(Nodding to* SHOWGIRL *as she passes)*
Hi, Cookie. I really dig that dress, baby.

ART
Things can always get worst, Pan.

PANDORA
Oh, you're one of those? How can they? Just lost my job. This was to keep us goin' until you guys turned up somethin' big, and I didn't even get paid for the last two weeks so I know this just means another great big zero.

ART
What do you think will happen now?

PANDORA
I don't know . . . the job Curt's got planned can't be pulled off until three more days and in a week we got to have all our money together for the restitution and juice . . . not to mention the goin' away money. And I'm not even goin' ta get paid for the gig.

ART
Haven't you got any now?

PANDORA
Just a couple of hundred, but we can't go into that. Got to hold on to it. We wouldn't eat if we didn't have to. We got to hold on to every cent.

BARTENDER *(In shadows)*
Do you want that scotch with anything?

(DRUMMER *momentarily breaks out of position)*

DRUMMER
I ain't finished talkin' yet, Chico.

BARTENDER
Just a minute, man.

(MAMMA *breaks out of position and goes to* PANDORA)

MAMMA
Lend me a dime, Pan. I got to call Shaky.

PANDORA *(Fishing in her outsized purse)*
You got somethin' workin', baby?

MAMMA
Yeah. Slim's gonna get somethin' from Shaky.

PANDORA
That's workin'.
(She gives MAMMA *a coin.* MAMMA *enters the shadows and walks to the rear of the club.* PANDORA *notices* ART *looking at her)*
Forget about her. Shaky's got her up tight. All you could do is play young lover a little. You can't support her habit, Art.

ART
She can't have a habit if she's just hit the street.

PANDORA
She's got one. What do you think they came in high on? In a couple more days she'll be hooked as bad as before. Shaky'll see to that.

ART
What does she do it for?

PANDORA
What does . . .? Awww, man . . . what kinda question
is that? I thought you knew somethin', baby.

ART
I tried to ask an honest question, Pan.

PANDORA
Is it an honest question when you don't have anything
to go by to compare her experience with yours?

ART
I don't know. Is it?

PANDORA
Do you know how it feels havin' somebody paw all
over you every day?

ART
Well, no . . .

PANDORA
Then you don't know that she has to use that stuff to
put off the reality of it happen'n?

ART
Oh, I see.

PANDORA *(Bitter)*
Yeah, you see. Do you see her givin' up her body every
day and murdering herself every day? Is that what
the world has brought to her, Art? That's all she can
look forward to each day . . . killin' herself with that
needle by inches. She has her fix, and maybe a bust,
and she has keepin' her man. She just takes her fixes
to get through the day and Shaky keeps her on it so
she'll need him more.

ART
That's too bad.

PANDORA
Wait a minute, Art. Don't sing no sad songs for that woman, you understand? She's not askin' for your pity. She's a real woman in some ways and she won't let you take it away from her by your pity. She'd spit on your pity.

ART *(Annoyed)*
And you?

(Lights change)

PANDORA *(Fantasy)*
And me? . . . Well, I ain't no whore . . . I'm just makin' this money so Curt and me can get on our feet. One day we gonna own property and maybe some businesses when we get straight . . . and out of this town.

ART
In Buffalo?

PANDORA
Maybe if we decide to stay there, but I'm really an entertainer. I'll show you my act one day . . . and Curt's got a good mind. He's a good hustler but he's givin' that up after a while. He can be anything he wants.

(Lights change)

ART
What does he want?

PANDORA
He wants what I want.

ART
How do you know?

PANDORA
He tells me . . . We talk about it all the time.

ART
Can you be sure?

PANDORA
Sure?

ART
Yeah . . . like Mamma's sure she'll always get her fix
and her bail paid.

PANDORA
You little smooth-faced punk . . . wha' . . .

ART *(Cutting)*
Some guys are really lucky.

PANDORA
Kiss my ass, sucker!

ART
Curt and Shaky are really into something.

PANDORA
Yeah! Because they're men!

ART
Is that what bein' a man is, bein' lucky?

PANDORA
No. It's from gettin' what you want.

ART
And how do you get what you want, Pan?

PANDORA
You go after it.

ART
And after you have it?

PANDORA
Then maybe it's yours and you can do whatever you
want with it.

ART
And what if I wanted you, Pandora?

PANDORA *(Three-beat pause)*
You don't have enough to give me, Art. What could
you give me that would make things better for me?

ART
I'm not a giver, Pan. I'm a taker.

> (*Lights go up evenly. Figures become animated
> and resume activities. The* BARTENDER *pours
> drinks and nods to grumbling* MUSICIANS
> *and to* CURT. *A* CUSTOMER *goes to jukebox
> and drops coin in. "Parisian Thoroughfare"
> plays. The* SHOWGIRL, *in thin robe revealing
> skimpy costume, walks from the rear and takes
> seat beside* CUSTOMER *she entered with.*
> MAMMA TOO TIGHT *goes to the table and
> sits)*

MAMMA (*Brightly*)
What you guys been talkin' 'bout so long?

PANDORA
Nothin' much, why?

MAMMA
Oh nuthin' . . . just thought I'd ask. But the way you
and ole fuzz wuzz was goin' at it and lookin' at each
other . . .

PANDORA
Looks can't hurt you, Mamma, but your big mouth can.

MAMMA (*Fake surprise*)
Pan . . . I didn't mean . . .

PANDORA
I'm sure you didn't, Mamma!

MAMMA (*Now hurt*)
Now listen, Pan. If you can't take a little teasin' . . .
What's wrong with you? This is my first day home and
you been on my ass all the time. Girl . . . you been the
best friend I ever had, but lighten up.

PANDORA
Awww, Mamma . . . let's not you and me start in actin'
flaky . . .

ART
Would you like a drink, Mamma?

MAMMA *(Pleased)*
Yeah . . . but you can't pry Chico from behind that bar.

> (ART *stands and places hand upon* MAMMA's *shoulder*)

ART
That's okay. Just sit.
> *(He goes to bar and stands beside* CURT, *who has his back to him, drinking and brooding)*

MAMMA *(To* PANDORA)
Hey, he's so nice.

PANDORA
See . . . I told you I wasn't tryin' to steal your little playmate.

MAMMA *(Serious)*
If I didn't know you was kiddin' I wouldn't take that, Pan.

PANDORA
You wouldn't? . . . Well, I wasn't kiddin', broad!

MAMMA *(Half-rising)*
Hey, check yourself, girl. This is me! Remember? Mamma Too Tight. Don't you know me? Li'l ole Queenie Bell Mack from Biloxi, Mississippi.

PANDORA
Okay. Sit down before you trip over yourself. I know who you are.

MAMMA *(Sitting)*
And I know you too, baby. Remember I was the one who was there those times so many yesterdays ago. Remember? I was there with you holding your hand in those dark, little lonely rooms all them nights that your man was out on a job . . . Remember how we

shivered together, girl? Remember how we cried together each time he got busted and sent away again?
. . . I'm your friend, baby . . . and you actin' like this
to me?

PANDORA *(Genuine)*
I'm sorry, Mamma. It's just that Art. He's different.
Everything seems different when he's around.

MAMMA
I think I know what you mean, Pan. I think I know . . .

> *(Lights dim; color-wheel still throws pastel
> shadows. CURT and ART stand in spot at end
> of bar. In the shadows there are rustles from
> the other people and lighted cigarettes arc
> through the gloom toward mouths which suck at
> them like spiders draining fireflies. CURT turns)*

CURT
Hey, Art. Sorry to put you through all this hassle but
some bad shit is goin' down, man. I'm really gettin'
worried . . . If things keep breakin' bad like this . . .

ART
Don't worry about me, Curt. I'm just along for the
ride. Try and get yourself together. It don't matter to
me what you have to go through to get yourself
straight, man. Just work it on out.

> *(Spot off ART and CURT. Spot on SHOWGIRL
> and CUSTOMER)*

CUSTOMER
How 'bout it, sugar?

SHOWGIRL
Are you kiddin', man?

CUSTOMER *(Whining)*
Well, Christ . . . twenty-five bucks . . . What's it lined
with . . . gold or somethin'?

SHOWGIRL
You see those two broads over at that table?

(Lights on PANDORA *and* MAMMA*)*

CUSTOMER
Yeah. You suggestin' that I hit on them?

SHOWGIRL
Yeah. Do that. The one in the black dress won't even speak to you unless you're ready to leave a hundred or more . . . and besides . . . She has to like your type first. The other one might consider it for fifty.

CUSTOMER
Who's the girl in the black dress?

SHOWGIRL
That's *Pandora.* She headlines the Revue. You have to give her twenty bucks just to get her phone number. So why don't you go hit on her?

(Lights off. Spot on BARTENDER*)*

BARTENDER
You call yourselves artists and then you want me to bleed for you? What kinda crap is that?

DRUMMER *(In shadows)*
Listen, you jive-time whisky-pourer. We are artists and I don't care what you call us or how you bleed. It's cats like you and your boss who make us all the time have to act like thugs, pimps and leeches to just make it out here in this world.

BARTENDER
So why ya tellin' me? So make it some other way!

PIANO PLAYER *(In shadows)*
It's just impossible to talk to you people . . . it's just impossible to be heard any more.

(Spot off BARTENDER. *Spot on* CURT *and* ART*)*

CURT

Yeah . . . when I first met her, Art. You should of
seen her. It was a joint somethin' like this . . .

> (Light off; spot picks up PANDORA standing
> in the door looking younger, nervous. CURT
> crosses stage to meet her as he speaks.

> Entering light)

She was just eighteen . . . had the prettiest little pair
of tits poking right out at me . . . sharp enough to put
your eyes out.

> (He takes PANDORA in his arms and kisses her
> violently. She resists but he is overwhelming)

PANDORA (Young voice)

I beg your pardon, mister.

CURT

I said that you're beautiful . . . that I want you . . .
that you are mine forever . . . that it will always be
this way for you, for you are mine.

> (He brutally subdues her. Her hair falls across
> her face. Her face has that expression that pris-
> oners sometimes have when they are shifted
> without prior explanation from an old cell to an
> unfamiliar cell equally as old)

PANDORA

Are you the man I'm to love?

CURT (Dragging her into the shadows)

Don't talk of something you'll never know anything
about . . .

> (They speak from the shadows now, facing the
> audience)

PANDORA

I can't love you? I can't love you if I even wanted? . . .

CURT

You are mine . . . my flesh . . . my body . . . you are
in my keeping.

PANDORA
Is it so much to ask for . . . just to be your woman?

CURT
You will do as I say . . . your flesh, your soul, your spirit is at my command . . . I possess you . . .

PANDORA
First there were others . . . now there is you . . . always, always the same for me . . .

(Lights change)

CURT (*In shadows, walking toward* **ART**)
Yeah . . . she was ready . . . has always been.

(Spot on **ART**. **CURT** *enters light)*

ART
Pandora's a beautiful girl, Curt. You're lucky, man, to have her. I envy you.

CURT
Thanks, Art.

ART
Don't mention it, don't mention it at all.

(Lights go down. Come up with **SHAKY** *sitting at the table with* **MAMMA** *and* **PANDORA**)

SHAKY
What's happen'n, baby?

MAMMA
Nothin' yet, Shaky. Give me time. The joint ain't even open yet.

SHAKY
Don't take too long, woman.

MAMMA
Give me time, Shaky. Why you got to come on so strong, man? You know I always take care of busi-

ness. You know I got to get used to it again. Didn't I set up that thing between you and Slim?

SHAKY
Yeah, baby. But that's my department. You take care of business on your side of the street.

(The BASS PLAYER *comes over to the table.*

To BASS PLAYER)
Let's take a walk, poppa.

BASS
After you, Shake Shake.

MAMMA
I'll be here, Shaky.

SHAKY
Let's hope you're either here or there . . . okay?

MAMMA
Shaky . . . you're goin' too fast. Don't push me so hard.

SHAKY *(Leaving)*
Tonight, baby. One hundred stone cold dollars, baby.

(Light on SHOWGIRL *and* CUSTOMER)

SHOWGIRL
They're alone. Why not now?

CUSTOMER
Okay . . . okay . . . twenty-five you get . . . after the show tonight.

(Lights off; spot on CURT *and* ART)

CURT
When I saw you in action, Art, I said to myself I could really use that kid. Man, you're like a little brother to me now, man. I watch the way you act around people. You think on your feet and study them like a good gambler does. You're like me in a lot of ways. Man, we're a new breed, ya know. Renegades. Rebels.

There's no rules for us . . . we make them as we break them.

ART
Sounds kinda romantic, Curt.

CURT
And why shouldn't it? Man, this ain't a world we built so why should we try to fit in it? We have to make it over the best we can . . . and we are the ones to do it. We are, man, we are!

(*Spot on* MAMMA)

MAMMA
I don't know why I'm this way . . . I just am. Is it because my name is different and I am different? Is it because I talk like a spade?

PANDORA (*From shadows*)
Take a look at that! Just because this white broad's been hangin' out with us for a couple of years she's goin' ta blame that bad talk on us.

(*Light on table.*

To MAMMA)
When you brought your funky ass from Mississippi, woman, we couldn't even understand you . . . sheeet . . . we taught you how to speak, if anything!

MAMMA (*Out at audience*)
All I know is that I'm here and that's where I'm at . . . and I'll be here until somethin' happens . . . I wish Shaky wouldn't push me so . . . I want to be good for him . . . I want him to be my man and care about me a little . . .

(ART *brings* MAMMA *her drink.* CURT *sits with him at the table*)

CURT (*To* PANDORA)
Don't look so pissed off, honey.

PANDORA
Why shouldn't I? Everything's gone wrong.

(CURT *stands and takes* PANDORA's *arm*)

CURT
C'mere, baby. Let me talk to you.

(They walk into the shadows)

ART
Just saw Shaky. He didn't stay long.

MAMMA
Nawh. He's gone to take care of some business. Wants me to stay here and take care of mine.

ART
I guess that's what you should do, then.

MAMMA
Should I? He's rushin' me too fast, that's what he's doin'. He knows I take a little time gettin' right inside before I can go back to work, but he's pushin' me. It's Curt's and Pan's fault . . . they're desperate for money and they're pressin' Shaky.

ART
Maybe you should try and talk to him or to Curt.

MAMMA
It wouldn't do any good!

ART
It wouldn't? If you were my girl I'd listen to what you had to say.

MAMMA
Oh, man, knock off the bullshit!

ART
But I would, really.

MAMMA *(Hesitant)*
You would? I bet you're full of shit.

ART
Sure I would. I look young but I know what you need
. . . and I know what you want.

MAMMA *(Giggling)*
You do?
　　　(Peering over her glass)
What do I need and want, fuzz wuzz?

ART
Understanding.

MAMMA
What!

ART *(Soft)*
Understanding.

MAMMA
Sheeet . . .

ART *(Softer)*
Understanding.

　　　(Lights down; spot on CURT *and* PANDORA*)*

PANDORA
I'm gettin' fed up with this shit, Curt. We seem to be
goin' backwards, not forward.

CURT
I know that, baby. But things will get straightened out.
You know it has to. When the job . . .

PANDORA *(Cutting)*
The job! Yeah . . . it better be somethin', Curt, or
you're in some big trouble . . . We're both in some big
trouble . . . what'd I do without you?

CURT
If anything happens, baby . . . let Art take care of
things . . .

PANDORA
Art?

CURT
Yeah.

PANDORA *(Afraid)*
But I'm your woman, remember?

CURT
He's like a little brother to me. I've already spoken to him about it . . . you can get a real gig in a show or somethin' and share an apartment with him. He'll look out for you while I'm away. Go up to Frisco and wait for me . . . Art's got a head and he can look after things until I get out . . . then things will be okay again. But that's if the worst happens and we don't get the juice money . . .

PANDORA *(Struck)*
You think that much of him, Curt?

CURT
I told you he's like my brother, baby. I've been waitin' a long time for a real cat to come along . . . we're on our way now . . .

(Lights lower; spot on table as SHAKY *enters)*

SHAKY *(To* ART*)*
Hey, what you say your name was?

ART *(Smiling, holding out his hand)*
It's Art, Shaky, you know I met . . .

SHAKY *(Cutting)*
Yeah, I know . . . what you doin' takin' up my old lady's time?

(BASS PLAYER *enters)*

ART
I was only sittin' here and bought her a drink. She rode over in my car with Curt and Pan.

SHAKY
That's what I mean, man . . . takin' up her time.

MAMMA
Shaky . . . stop it! He wasn't doin' nothin' . . . he's a
friend of Curt's, man . . .

SHAKY
Shut up!

MAMMA
You don't understand . . .
> *(He slaps her.* ART *grabs his arm and pushes
> him sprawling across a chair.* SHAKY *regains
> his balance and begins to lunge but is caught by*
> CURT)

CURT
Hey, cool it, man! What's goin' on?

SHAKY
This little punk friend of yours doesn't like what I
do with my woman.

BASS PLAYER
Why don't you forget it, Shaky. If it had been me I
would of done the same thing. Forget it. It ain't worth
it.

MAMMA *(Scared)*
He don't understand.

SHAKY
You'll see what I understand when we get home, bitch!

ART *(Putting out his hand)*
I'm sorry, man. It was my fault. I had . . .

> (SHAKY *knocks* ART's *hand aside and turns,
> being led toward the door by the* MUSICIAN)

SHAKY *(To* ART)
I'll see you later.

CURT
Hey, Shaky. C'mere, man. It don't mean nothin'.

(They exit. PANDORA takes a seat. CURT goes to the bar and answers the questions of the MUSICIANS and the BARTENDER. The SHOWGIRL goes to the rear of the club and the CUSTOMER orders another drink)

MAMMA
He just don't understand . . . he can't understand and he can't give me any understanding . . .

PANDORA
Who don't understand, Mamma?

MAMMA
Shaky . . . he just don't understand . . . he should try and understand me more.

PANDORA
Girl, you so stoned you're not makin' any sense. He understands, Mamma. He understands you perfectly.

MAMMA
He can't, Pan. He can't or I wouldn't feel this way about him now.

ART
Maybe you're changin'.

PANDORA
Oh, man, you're full of it!

ART
You're cynical but not that hard, Pandora.

PANDORA
Man, I've seen it all. I don't have to be hard . . . I just use what I know.

ART
Have you seen everything, Pan?

PANDORA
Yes!

ART
Then you've seen me before?

PANDORA *(Staring)*
Yeah . . . I've seen you before. There's a you standin'
on every corner with his hands in his pockets and his
fly half unzipped . . . there's a you in every drunk tank
in every city . . . there's a you sniffin' around moochin'
drinks and kissin' ass and thinkin' he's a make-out
artist. Yeah . . . I've seen you before, punk!

MAMMA
He just don't understand . . .

ART
No, you've never seen me before, Pandora. I'm goin' a
tell you something.

PANDORA *(Sarcastic)*
What are you goin' a tell me, Art?

ART
That I'm goin' a change your life.

PANDORA
What!!!

> *(Lights go up with a startling flash. DEENY
> and the BOUNCER, Pete, enter. DEENY, in
> black glasses, sports an ascot and a cummerbund
> under his sport coat. In the thin dress she entered
> in, the SHOWGIRL walks from the rear and
> takes a seat beside the CUSTOMER. MAMMA
> TOO TIGHT stands and CURT nearly bowls over
> a CUSTOMER on his way to meet DEENY in
> center stage in front of PANDORA's table. PAN-
> DORA jumps to her feet beside MAMMA, fol-
> lowed by ART)*

CURT
Deeny!

> *(The BASS PLAYER enters, and the DRUM-
> MER and PIANO PLAYER hurry over. Behind
> the bar the BARTENDER stands tensed; the
> BASS PLAYER climbs upon the stage and be-
> gins zippering his bass fiddle into its cloth bag)*

DEENY
Keep it, Curt! I don't want to hear it. I just came
from the union and I've taken all the crap I'm gonna
. . . the show's closed.

(Chorus of yells)

CURT
Deeny, what you take us for?

PANDORA
Hey, man . . . let's go in the back and talk . . .

DRUMMER *(Pushing his way around the* PIANO
PLAYER)
Yeah, Deeny, I want to talk to you!

DEENY
I just don't want to hear it from any of you. *Okay?* . . .
Okay! Now everybody . . . this club is closin'. Ya hear?
Everybody out inside of ten minutes . . . understand?
This is my property. Get off it inside of ten minutes or
I'm callin' the cops . . . your things and you out . . . hit
the street . . . that means everybody!

*(Another chorus of yells from nearly everyone.
The* CUSTOMERS *hurry out the exit and the*
SHOWGIRL *joins the group)*

BASS PLAYER *(To other* MUSICIANS)
Hey, fellas, I'm splittin' . . . what about you?

*(*MAMMA *turns and goes over to him)*

DRUMMER
Man, what about my pay?

DEENY
Take your bitchin' to the union, fellah. They instigated
this hassle.

PANDORA
We don't know nothin' 'bout no union, Deeny . . .

DEENY *(Sarcastic)*
I know you don't, sugar. But you girls should get or-

ganized . . . try to get paid hourly and get off the quota system and you'd . . .

CURT
Watch your mouth, mathafukker!

BOUNCER
You'd better watch yours!

DEENY *(To* BARTENDER)
Hey, Chico, call the cops! You just can't reason with some jerks! Call them now!

(*The* BARTENDER *dials*)

PANDORA *(To* CURT)
What we gonna do, baby? . . .

CURT
Quiet!

PANDORA
But your case, honey . . .

BARTENDER *(On phone)*
Yeah . . . there's trouble at the Strip Club on Western . . . yeah . . .

(DEENY *tries to push his way past but* CURT *blocks him. The* BOUNCER *moves to shove* CURT *out of the way but* ART *steps in as the four confront each other, and the girls back off. The* PIANO PLAYER *has coaxed the* DRUM-MER *to join the* BASS PLAYER *upon the stage, packing away his equipment. At a run, the* SHOWGIRL *rushes to the rear of the club as the* BARTENDER *hangs up the phone.*

As the other MUSICIANS *pack up, the* PIANO PLAYER *comes back to the group)*

PIANO
Deeny, you just can't do this. This ain't right about us. We stuck by you for below scale wages, riskin' our own necks with the union to keep you in business, until you

got on your feet. And still we never got paid on time. Now I hear you gonna put some names in here and clean up on the rep we made for you.

BOUNCER
Shut up, mister. You're not supposed to be here right now, remember?

PANDORA *(Furious)*
You owe me for two and a half weeks, man!

DEENY *(Trying to get by again)*
Sorry, baby. Come around sometime and maybe we can work out somethin'.

CURT
I know why you doin' this, Deeny. Don't pull that union shit on me! You want all the girls to work for you . . . on the block like tramps for ten and fifteen dollars a trick. Pan, Mamma and all the other broads. I'd die before I'd let you put my woman on the street for ten tricks a day. Why you got to be so fuckin' greedy, man? You ain't right! You already got six girls now.

BOUNCER
Just say he has taste and discrimination, Curt. You know he wants your old lady because . . .

DEENY *(Cutting)*
Shut up all of you! And are you goin' to get out of my way?

MAMMA *(From bandstand)*
Deeny. Who you think you are?

DEENY *(To MAMMA)*
You know who I am, you stupid country cunt. And if you want to stay on the streets and keep that junkie ole man of yours cool, just keep your mouth out of this! That way you won't get your legs broke and . . .

CURT *(Cutting)*
I know why you doin' this, Deeny.

(SHAKY *enters. The* SHOWGIRL *rushes from the rear with costumes in arms and exits, speaking to no one)*

SHAKY
Did I hear somebody say they gonna break Mamma's legs?

(There is general bedlam with shouts and near screaming)

DRUMMER *(Exiting)*
I'm goin' ta take this farther than to the union, Deeny!

BOUNCER
You can take it to your mother, punk!

(DRUMMER drops equipment and lunges toward BOUNCER but PIANO PLAYER grabs him and holds. BASS PLAYER helps)

BASS PLAYER *(Exiting with DRUMMER)*
Hey, Deeny, you're wrong! You're dead wrong, man!

PIANO *(To CURT and PANDORA)*
Cool it. Let's all split. This ain't nothin' but a big bust.

(It becomes suddenly quiet and the BARTENDER, a club in hand, comes around the bar and stands behind CURT and ART. SHAKY stands to the side of DEENY and the BOUNCER. MAMMA is on the bandstand, wide-eyed, and PANDORA is downstage glowering at her enemies.

Leaving)
I'll see you guys.
(Seeing SHAKY)
Hey, man. It ain't worth it.

SHAKY
I'll get in touch with you, okay?

PIANO
C'mon, man. I don't like what I see.

SHAKY
Make it! Be a good friend and make it.

> (PIANO PLAYER *exits. It is even more quiet. Very low, from somewhere outside, the theme is heard as each group eyes the other and tenses*)

PANDORA *(Spitting it out, violent as unsuspected spit splattering a face)*
Fuck you, Deeny! Fuck you! Fuck you! *Fuck you!*

DEENY *(Frenzied)*
You little trampy bitch . . . you . . .

> (CURT *smashes him in the mouth as he reaches for* PANDORA. DEENY *falls back beside the table, grabs a glass and hurls it into* CURT's *face, shattering it.* CURT *launches himself upon him and pummels* DEENY *to the floor.*
>
> *Meanwhile, the* BOUNCER *and* ART *fight in center stage.* SHAKY *is struck almost immediately from behind by the* BARTENDER's *club.* ART, *seeing the* BARTENDER *advancing on* CURT's *rear, breaks away and desperately kicks out at the* BARTENDER. *With a screech he doubles over and grabs his groin. The* BOUNCER *seizes* ART *from behind, about the throat, in an armlock, and begins strangling him.* PANDORA, *who has taken off her shoes after kicking* DEENY *several times as* CURT *beats him upon the floor, attacks the* BOUNCER *from behind and repeatedly strikes him about the head with her shoe heels. The* BOUNCER *loosens his grip on* ART *and grabs* PANDORA *and punches her. She falls.* ART, *gasping, reaches down for the* BARTENDER's *dropped club, picks it up and turns and beats the* BOUNCER *to the floor.*
>
> *All the while* MAMMA TOO TIGHT *screams.*

With face bloodied from splintered glass, CURT *has beaten* DEENY *into unconsciousness and staggers over and pulls* PANDORA *up.*

Sirens, screeches and slamming car doors are heard outside. Shouts)

CURT *(Towing* PANDORA)
C'mon, Art! Pull yourself together. The cops are here.

(ART *staggers over to* SHAKY *and tries to lift him but he is too weak.* MAMMA, *crying and screaming, jumps from the bandstand and pulls at* SHAKY.

Heading for the rear)
He's too heavy, Art. Leave him. Grab Mamma and let's get out the back way. *Move! C'mon, man, move!*

(Dazed, but following orders, ART *grabs* MAMMA's *arms and struggles with her)*

MAMMA *(Resisting)*
No! No! I can't leave him like that!

CURT *(Exiting)*
Bring her, Art. Out the back way to the car.

MAMMA *(Being dragged out by* ART)
My first day out . . . my first day . . .

(They exit and immediately the stage blackens, then the tumble of running feet, then)

VOICE
Christ!

(More heavy running, then stop)

Hey, call a couple of ambulances . . . Emergency!

CURTAIN

ACT III

SCENE 1

Time: Three days later. Afternoon.

Scene: CURT's apartment. He and RICH play chess as in Act I. The bed is lowered and MAMMA TOO TIGHT sleeps with the covers pulled up to her chin as if she is cold. The radio is off and the California sunshine glistens in the clean room. The room looks sterile, unlived in and motel-like without the lighting of the first act.

CURT wears two Band-Aids upon his face, one upon his forehead, the other on the bridge of his nose.

CURT *(Bored)*
It'll be mate in two moves, Rich. Do you want to play it out?

RICH
Nawh, man. I ain't up to it.

CURT *(Sitting back)*
The last three days have just taken everything out of me, man.

RICH
Yeah. They been pretty rough.

> (CURT *stands, stretches and walks across the stage)*

Hey, man. Is there any more beer?

CURT
Nawh. Pan and Art's bringing some in with them when they come.

RICH *(Muttering)*
Yeah . . . when they get here.

CURT *(Noticing* RICH's *tone)*
What did you say, man?

RICH
Oh. Nothin', man.

CURT *(Sharply)*
You're a liar . . . I heard what you said!

RICH *(Sullen)*
I ain't goin' a be many more of them liars, Curt.

CURT *(Gesturing)*
Awww, man. Forget it . . . you know how I feel with Deeny in a coma from his concussion for the past three days and me not knowin' if he's goin' ta press charges finally or die.

RICH
Yeah, man. I'm a bit edgy myself. Forget about what I said.

(CURT *returns to the couch and sprawls back)*

CURT
But I'd like to know what you meant by it, Rich.

RICH *(Seeing no way out)*
Now, Curt. You and I been friends since we were young punks stealin' hub caps and tires together, right? Remember that time you, me and the guys gang-banged that Pechuco broad? . . . And the Dog Town boys came up and we had that big rumble and they killed Sparky?

CURT *(Sensing something coming)*
How can I forget it? . . . I served my first stretch behind it for stabbin' that Mexican kid, Manuel.

RICH
Yeah. That was a good time ago and Manuel ain't no kid no more . . . he got killed in Korea.

CURT
Yeah. But, tell me. What do you have to say, good
buddy?

RICH *(Pausing, then serious)*
It's about this guy Art and Pandora, man.

CURT
What do you mean, man?

RICH
Man . . . I don't mean there's anything goin' on yet . . .
but each afternoon he's taken Pandora out for the past
three days they been gettin' back later . . . and . . .

CURT
And what, Rich!

RICH
And the way she looks at him, Curt.

CURT *(Disgusted and angry)*
Awww, man . . . I thought I knew you better.

RICH
Well, I told you that I didn't think they were doin'
anything really.

CURT
But, what? That he drives her up to Sunset Strip to
keep her dates with the big tricks . . . you know how
much dough she brings back, man?

RICH *(Resolutely)*
Yeah, man. Sometimes over a hundred dollars for one
trick.

CURT
So you can't hurry those people for that kinda bread,
man.

RICH *(Trying to be understood)*
But I wasn't talkin' about the tricks, Curt. I don't
think they're holdin' back any money on you.

CURT
Then what are you talkin' 'bout?

RICH
About that little jive-ass square gettin' next to your woman, that's what!

CURT
Now listen, Rich. We're friends and all that, but that little jive-ass square as you call him is just like a brother to me . . . and we been in some tighter things than you and me will ever be in.

RICH *(Obviously hurt)*
Well, forget it!

CURT
No, let's not forget it. You're accusing my wife of jivin' around on me. You know that Pan's the straightest broad you'll ever find. That's why I married her. You know if we couldn't have gotten another man that she would have gone on the job and been as good as most men. She and I are a team. What could she gain by messin' 'round on me with my ace buddy?

RICH
Forget it, I said.

CURT
Nawh, Rich. I don't want to. I know what's really buggin' you. Ever since Shaky got busted at the Club and they found all that smack on him you been buggin' Mamma to be your woman 'cause you know that with Shaky's record he won't be hittin' the streets again for at least ten years. But you're wrong on two counts, 'cause we're bailin' out Shaky tonight and takin' him with us; and Mamma don't want you cause she wants Art, but he don't go for her.

RICH *(Getting to his feet)*
I'll see you, man. Between your broad and that cat you can't think any more!

(CURT *reaches for* RICH's *shirt front;* RICH
throws his hands off)

Take it easy, Curt. You already won a close one this week. And your guardian angel ain't around to sneak punch people.

(CURT *stares at him and steps back*)

MAMMA *(From bag)*
Hey, what's all that shoutin' about?

CURT
Nothin', baby. Rich and I are just crackin' jokes.

MAMMA *(Sitting up)*
Curt, I wonder if . . .

CURT
No, Mamma. You can't have no fix. Remember what I told you? You don't turn no tricks in town 'cause you're hot behind Shaky's bust so you don't need any heroin, right? You're on holiday and besides, you're full of codein now . . . that's enough . . .

MAMMA
But I would be good if I could get some. I wouldn't worry about Shaky so much and I'd feel . . .

CURT
You just come out of the joint clean, Mamma. You don't need anything but to keep cool.

MAMMA *(Pouting)*
But I got the sixteen hundred dollars that Shaky had stashed at our pad. I could buy it okay, Curt.

CURT
Forget it. That money is with the other, broad. We all takin' a trip with that. Besides . . . Shaky had over two thousand bucks' worth of stuff in the pad and we sellin' it tonight so we can bail him out so he can leave with us . . .

(MAMMA *jumps out of bed in a thin gown*)

MAMMA *(Delighted)*
You are? Then he'll be home soon?

CURT
Yeah. Then we all make it before Deeny comes out of his coma or croaks. Now get back in bed before Rich grabs you!

MAMMA *(Playful)*
Rich, you better not. Shaky will be home soon.

RICH *(Teasing)*
Sheeet, woman. I don't care about old ass Shaky. C'mon, baby, why don't you get yourself a young stud?

MAMMA *(Getting in bed)*
When I get one it won't be you.

RICH *(Serious)*
Then who?

CURT *(Mutters)*
I told Art and Pan that we need the car this evening to drop off the stuff. After that it'll be time to get ready for the job.

RICH *(Bitterly, to* MAMMA)
So he's got to you, too.

MAMMA
Nobody's got to me. What'chou talkin' 'bout, Rich? Art's been stayin' over to Shaky and my place for the last couple of nights while I stayed here. How can he get . . .

RICH *(Cutting)*
How did you know I was talkin' about Art?

MAMMA
'Cause you got Art on the brain, that's why!

CURT
I thought we dropped that, Rich.

RICH *(To* MAMMA*)*
If you're goin' a get somebody young . . . get a man
. . . not some little book-readin' faggot . . .

MAMMA *(Red-faced to* RICH*)*
Oh, go fuck yourself, man!
  (She covers her head)

RICH
Okay, man. We got a lot to do tonight, so I'll lay off.

  *(Through the back curtain the outside kitchen
  door can be seen opening. Dusk is come and* ART
  enters first with a large bag; PANDORA *follows, closes the door and purposely bumps
  against him as she passes.*

  She wears dark glasses, her pants and boots)

ART
Hey, you almost made me drop this! Where should I
put it?

  *(*PANDORA *enters front room smiling)*

PANDORA
Hi, honey. Hello, Rich.
  (She walks over to CURT, *kisses him and places
  money in his hand)*

CURT
Hey, pretty baby.
  *(He pulls her to him, gives her an extended kiss
  and breaks it, looking over* PANDORA*'s shoul-
  der at* RICH, *who looks away)*
Everything okay?

PANDORA
Smooth as Silky Sullivan.

  (In the kitchen ART *is taking items from the
  bag.*

  CURT *hands back the money to* PANDORA*)*

CURT
Here, Pan, put this in the box with the rest.

PANDORA
Okay.
> *(She walks past bed and looks down)*

What's wrong with Mamma?

CURT
Rich's been tryin' to love her up.

RICH
She won't go for my program, baby.

PANDORA *(Entering the kitchen)*
That's too bad . . . you better cultivate some charm, Rich.

RICH
Yeah, that's what's happen'n. I'm not one of the lucky ones . . . some people don't need it.

PANDORA *(Going to* ART*)*
Let me take in the beer, Art. You put the frozen food in the refrigerator and the canned things in the cupboard.

> (ART *pulls her to him and kisses her.*
>
> *Taking breath)*

Hand me the glasses, will ya?

> *(They kiss again, she responding this time, then she pushes him away and begins fixing beer for* CURT *and* RICH*)*

CURT
Hey, Mamma. You want any beer?

MAMMA *(Under the cover)*
No, no.

> (PANDORA *serves* CURT *and* RICH, *then climbs the stairs and enters the dressing room.*
>
> ART *comes out of the kitchen)*

RICH
How you feel, Art?

ART
Okay. Hollywood's an interesting place. First job I ever had just drivin' somebody around.

CURT
Hope it's your last, Art. With this job tonight and my cut from sellin' Shaky's heroin we'll be just about in. Might even go into business back East.

ART
Yeah? I hope so.

CURT
We already got almost twenty-four hundred with Shaky's money we found at his place and the bread we've been able to hustle the last few days. After tonight we'll be set.

RICH
Yeah. After tonight you'll be set.

CURT *(Looking at RICH)*
It's too bad you won't come with us, Rich. But your share will fix you up out here okay.

RICH
Fix me up? Ha ha . . . I'll probably shoot that up in smack inside of several months . . . but if I make it I'll probably be lookin' you up in two more years when my probation's up. No use ruinin' a good thing. When I cut this town loose I want to be clean. I just hope all goes well with you.

ART *(Smiling)*
Why shouldn't it?

CURT
Yeah, Rich, why shouldn't it?

RICH
Funny things happen to funny-style people, ya know.

CURT
Yeah. Too bad you won't be comin' along . . . we need
a clown in our show.

(RICH *watches* ART *studying the chess game*)

RICH
Do you see anything I missed, good buddy?

ART
Oh. I don't know.

RICH
You know I seldom beat Curt. Why don't you play him?

ART *(Still looking at board)*
Maybe I will when we find time.

CURT
What would you have done from there, Art?

ART
It's according to what side I'm on.

CURT
You have the black. White's going to mate you in two
moves.

ART
He is?

RICH
Yeah. He is.

(ART *reaches over and picks up the black king*)

ART
Most kings need a queen to be most powerful but
others do the best they can.
(He places the king upon another square)
That's what I'd do, Rich.

CURT *(Perceiving)*
Yeah. I see . . . I see . . .

RICH
Say, why'd you move there? . . . He can't move now
. . . he can't put himself in check . . .

ART *(As RICH stares at him)*
Yeah, Rich?

CURT *(Matter-of-factly)*
A stalemate.

RICH *(Muttering)*
I should of seen that.
        (To ART)
How did you . . . why . . .

ART
When you play the game you look for any break you
can make.

CURT
We should play sometime, Art.

ART
I'm looking forward to it, Curt. But you name the
time.

CURT *(Standing)*
I'll do that. *Hey, Pandora!* We got to go!

> (PANDORA *comes to the top of the stairs. She
> has changed into a simple dress)*

PANDORA
We goin' some place?

CURT
I got to drop Shaky's stuff off and go down to the bail
bondsman and the lawyer. I want you to drive. C'mon,
Rich. Pan will sit in the car down the street in the
next block and you and me will walk up the street
talkin' about baseball, understand? On the corner of
Adams and Crenshaw we'll meet a man and hit a
grand slam.

RICH
Yeah, I hope so, brother.

CURT
It's trip time from here on in, baby.

PANDORA *(Excited)*
Wait until I get my coat.

CURT *(In good humor)*
Let's go, woman. It's eighty degrees outside and we
might be the hottest thing in L.A. but it just ain't that
warm. Let's go, now. See you, Art.
        (Going to ART)
Oh, I almost forgot the car keys.

ART *(Handing him the keys)*
See you guys.

CURT *(Hands keys to* PANDORA)
You'll watch the phone, okay?

ART
Sure, good buddy, I'll see to the phone.

CURT
If Mamma wakes up and wants a fix don't give in to
her.

ART
I'll try not to.

CURT *(Serious)*
I mean it, Art.

ART *(Smiling)*
I'm dead serious, man.

PANDORA
See you later, Art.

ART
See you later, Pan. Goodbye, Curt. Goodbye, Rich.

(The trio exits and **ART** *goes to the radio and switches it on. It plays the theme as he enters the kitchen and gets himself a beer. He comes from the kitchen drinking from the bottle and climbs the bathroom stairs. His shadow is seen lifting and then dialing. His voice is muffled by the music and by his whisper; nothing is understood.*

After the shadow hangs up, **ART** *returns to the living room and descends the stairs. He sits upon the bed and shakes* MAMMA TOO TIGHT)*

MAMMA *(Being shaken)*
Huh? I don't want any beer.

> *(*ART *shakes her once more. She uncovers her head)*

Oh, Art. It's you. Where's everybody?

> *(He doesn't answer, looks at her. Evening comes and the room blackens)*

I'm glad you woke me. I always like to talk to you but I guess I bug you since you don't say too much to me. Why ain't you sayin' nothin' now?

> *(Three-beat pause)*

ART *(Laughing)*
Ha ha ha . . . ha ha . . . Ma-Ma Too Tight! . . . ha ha ha . . .

MAMMA
You said it! Sometimes you have such a nice look on your face and now . . . you look different . . .
> *(Pause)*
. . . like you so happy you could scream . . . You never looked at me like this before, Art, never.

> *(In total blackness as the music plays)*

You said Shaky wouldn't be back? . . . He won't? . . . I don't care as long as you don't go away . . . You know

... you understand me. It's like you can look inside my head . . . Oh, how did you know? Just a little bit? More? You say I can have a fix anytime I want? . . . Oh! . . . You understand me, don'tcha? Don't let Curt know . . . you say don't worry about Curt . . . don't care what anybody thinks or says except you? . . .

(Silence, pause)

Oh I feel so good now . . . I didn't know but I was hoping . . . I didn't know, honey . . . *Oh, Art* . . . Ahhhh . . . now I can feel you oozing out of me . . . and I'm glad, so glad . . . it's good . . .

ACT III

SCENE 2

PANDORA leans against the kitchen door as the lights go up. The atmosphere of the first act is re-created by the lights and music. The bed has been put up and ART sits upon the couch. PANDORA has been crying and what can be seen of her face around her dark glasses appears shocked.

She walks to the center of the room and faces ART.

PANDORA
Art . . . Art . . . they got them. They got Curt and Rich . . . with all that stuff on them. The cops were waitin' on them. They busted them with all those narcotics . . . we'll never see them again.

ART *(Rising)*
We're hot, Pandora. We got to get out of town.

PANDORA
They got 'em, don't you hear me, Art? What can we do?

ART
Nothin' . . . we got to make it before Curt or Rich break, and the cops are kickin' that door in.

PANDORA
You said nothin'? But we . . . what do you mean? We got to do somethin'!
    (Crying)
We can't just let it happen to them . . . we got to do somethin' like Curt would do if it was one of us . . . Art! Art! *Don't just stand there!*

(He slaps her viciously, knocking off her glasses, exposing her blackened eyes)

ART *(Commanding)*
Get a hold of yourself, Pandora. You've had a bad experience.

(She holds her face and looks dazed)

Now listen to me. Mamma has gone over to her place to pack and as soon as she gets back we're all leaving.

PANDORA *(Dazed)*
Mamma is packin'? . . . Did Curt tell her to pack?

ART
You know he didn't. Now as soon as she gets here I want us to be packed, okay?

PANDORA
But . . . Art . . . packed . . . where we goin'?

ART
To Buffalo, baby. Where else?

PANDORA
To Buffalo?

ART
That's what I said. Now go up in your dressing room and get your case.

(A knock comes from the front door)

That's Mamma already . . . we're runnin' late, woman. C'mon, get a move on.
(He shoves her)
Move! Get a move on, Pandora!

(She stumbles over the first step, catches her balance and begins climbing.

ART *looks after her)*
Oh . . . Pandora . . .

(She turns and looks vacantly at him)

. . . Don't forget your box!

*(As she turns and climbs the last steps, ART
saunters to the radio as the knock sounds again.*

*Instantaneously, as he switches the radio off, the
stage is thrown in complete blackness)*

CURTAIN

Bette Howard as LOU, Gary Bolling as RAY, and Sonny Jim as CLIFF DAWSON in a scene from In the Wine Time. *(Photo courtesy of The New Lafayette Theatre.)*

IN THE
WINE TIME

to Janice

In the Wine Time was first produced at the New Lafayette Theatre on December 10, 1968. The production was directed by Robert Macbeth. Sets were designed by Roberta Raysor, lighting by Ernest Baxter and Richard Macbeth. The cast was as follows:

CLIFF DAWSON	Sonny Jim
LOU DAWSON, Cliff's wife	Bette Jean Howard
RAY, Lou's nephew	Gary Bolling
MISS MINNY GARRISON	Rosanna Carter
BUNNY GILLETTE	Helen Ellis
MRS. KRUMP	Voice of V. Rachman Cyrille
EDDIE KRUMP	Voice of Leopoldo Mandeville
BEATRICE	Roberta Raysor
TINY	Yvette Hawkins
SILLY WILLY CLARK	Whitman Mayo
RED	Kris Keiser
BAMA	George Miles
DORIS	Peggy A. Kirkpatrick
A POLICEMAN	Bill Lathan

In this production the characters of MR. KRUMP, THE GIRL, and some Derby Street Residents were omitted.

THE PROLOGUE

She passed the corner every evening during my last wine time, wearing a light summer dress with big pockets, in small ballerina slippers, swinging her head back and to the side all special-like, hearing a private melody singing in her head. I waited for her each dusk, and for this she granted me a smile, but on some days her selfish tune would drift out to me in a hum; we shared the smile and sad tune and met for a moment each day but one of that long-ago summer.

The times I would be late she lingered, in the sweating twilight, at the corner in the barber shop doorway, ignoring the leers and coughs from within, until she saw me hurrying along the tenement fronts. On these days her yellows and pinks and whites would flash out from the smoked walls, beckoning me to hurry hurry to see the lights in her eyes before they fleeted away above the single smile, which would turn about and then down the street, hidden by the little pretty head. Then, afterwards, I would stand before the shop refusing to believe the slander from within.

"Ray . . . why do you act so stupid?" Lou asked each day I arose to await the rendezvous.

"I don't know . . . just do, that's all," I always explained.

"Well, if you know you're bein' a fool, why do you go on moonin' out there in the streets for *that*? . . ."

"She's a friend of mine, Lou . . . she's a friend."

August dragged in the wake of July in steaming sequence of sun and then hell and finally sweltering night. The nights found me awake with Cliff and Lou and our bottles of port, all waiting for the sun to rise again and then to sleep in dozes during the miserable hours. And then for me to wake hustling my liquor money and then to wait on the corner for my friend to pass.

"What'd the hell you say to her, Ray?" Cliff asked.

"Nothin'."

"Nothing?"

"Nawh . . . nothin'."

"Do you ever try?"

"Nawh," I said.

"Why? She's probably just waiting for you to . . ."

"Nawh, she's not. We don't need to say anything to each other. We know all we want to find out."

And we would go on like that until we were so loaded our voices would crack and break as fragile as eggs and the subject would escape us, flapping off over the roofs like a fat pigeon.

Summer and Cliff and Lou and me together—all poured from the same brew, all hating each other and loving, and consuming and never forgiving—but not letting go of the circle until the earth swung again into winter, bringing me closer to manhood and the freedom to do all the things that I had done for the past three summers.

We were the group, the gang. Cliff and Lou entangled within their union, soon to have Baby Man, and Henrietta, and Stinky, and Debra, and maybe who knows who by now. Summer and me wrapped in our embrace like lovers, accepting each as an inferior, continually finding faults and my weaknesses, pretending to forgive though never forgetting, always at each other's vitals . . . My coterie and my friend . . .

She with the swinging head and flat-footed stance and the single smile and private song for me. She was missing for a day in the last week of summer.

I waited on the corner until the night boiled up from the pavements and the wine time approached too uncomfortably.

Cliff didn't laugh when learning of my loss; Lou stole a half a glass more than I should have received. The night stewed us as we blocked the stoop fighting for air and more than our shares of the port, while the bandit patrol cruised by as sinister as gods.

She was there waiting next day, not smiling nor humming but waving me near. I approached and saw my very own smile.

"I love you, little boy," she said.

I nodded, trying to comprehend.

"You're my little boy, aren't you?" She took my hand. "I have to go away but I wanted to tell you this before I left." She looked into my eyes and over my shaggy uncut hair. "I must be years older than you, but you look so much older than I. In two more years you won't be able to stop with only wine," she said. "Do you have to do it?"

"I don't know . . . just do, that's all," I explained.

"I'm sorry, my dear," she said. "I must go now."

"Why?"

"I just must."

"Can I go with you?"

She let go of my hand and smiled for the last time.

"No, not now, but you can come find me when you're ready."

"But where?" I asked.

"Out in the world, little boy, out in the world. Remember, when you're ready, all you have to do is leave this place and come to me, I'll be waiting. All you'll need to do is search!"

Her eyes lighted for the last time before hiding behind the pretty head, swinging then away from me, carrying our sorrowful, secret tune.

I stood listening to the barber shop taunts follow her into the darkness, watching her until the wicked city night captured her; then I turned back to meet autumn and Cliff and Lou in our last wine time, meeting the years which had to hurry hurry so I could begin the search that I have not completed.

ACT I

The people in this play are black except for the KRUMPS and the POLICEMAN.

Scene: Derby Street. A small side street of a large northern American industrial city, in the early 1950's.

At left, the houses stand together on one side of the street in unbroken relief, except for a tunnel-like alley which opens between the Krumps' and the Garrisons' houses, forming a low, two-storied canyon, the smoke-stained chimneys the pinnacles of the ridges. Four-letter words, arrow-pierced hearts and slangy street-talk, scrawled in haste, smear a wooden fence, painted green, across the narrow street. Tattered posters of political candidates wearing scribbled, smudged mustaches, circuses of seasons passed and fading, golden and orange snuff containers decorate the enclosure. Each building's front is dull red, not brick colored, but a grey- and violet-tinged red, the shade the paint becomes after successive seasons of assault by the city's smoke- and grit-ladened atmosphere. Precise white lines, the older ones yellowing, outline each brick of the walls, and every house has a squat stoop of five white stone steps.

A raised level, upstage right, between the fence and the houses, represents "The Avenue."

From within the DAWSONS' house black music of the period—called rhythm 'n blues by disc jockeys at that time—

is heard not too loudly, and continues throughout the play, interrupted only seldom by amusing, jive-talking commercials for used cars, televisions, appliances, hair straighteners and skin lighteners. Some of the recording stars of this season are King Pleasure, Johnnie Otis, Fats Domino, Little Esther, Ray Charles and "The Queen," Miss Dinah Washington. When MISS MINNY GARRISON raises her window gospel music can be heard.

At Rise: It is a sultry evening in late August. All the steps are occupied by members of the various Derby Street households.

At the end of the street, downstage, is a corner lighted by a streetlamp, the gas-burning variety found still then in some sections of Philadelphia, Baltimore, New York and Boston.

All lights are down but the corner streetlamp, though dim shadows of the people on the stoops can be seen carrying on their evening activities: talking, gossiping, playing checkers and cards, drinking sodas, wine and beer.

MR. KRUMP enters and stands at the streetlamp. He is very drunk.

Lights on the Krumps' doorstoop, the nearer to the corner.

The Krumps' front door opens and MRS. KRUMP leans out.

THE RADIO
And here we are folks . . . on a black juicy, jammin' 'n' groovin' hot August night . . . yeah . . . one of them nights fo' bein' wit' tha one ya loves . . .

MRS. KRUMP *(Strident, over the radio)*
Krumpy! What cha doin' on da corner? Hey, Krumpy!
Hey, Krumpy! . . . *Krumpy . . . Get the hell on over
here!*
>*(Light on third doorstoop)*

CLIFF
Heee . . . heee . . . look 'a ole man Krump work out.

>(BUNNY GILLETTE *and* DORIS *enter Derby
>Street at the corner and see* MR. KRUMP)

LOU
Hush up, Cliff.

CLIFF
Sheeet.

BUNNY GILLETTE
Look 'a there, Doris!

LOU
Be quiet, Cliff. Will ya, huh?

DORIS
Awww, shit, girl. That's nothin' . . . it just that goddamn Mr. Krump again . . . drunk out of his fucken'
mind.

THE RADIO
It's eighty-two degrees . . . maaan, that's hot-oh-rooney
. . . yeah, burnin' up this evenin' . . . red hot! . . .
Ouch! . . . But we're cool on the Hep Harrison red-hot,
up-tight, out-a-sight weather lookout indicator. That's
eighty-two degrees . . . that's eight two out there . . .
And here's a cool number that will hit you right where
you're at . . . for your listenin' pleasure . . .

>(MRS. KRUMP *has stepped to the center of
>Derby Street and calls up to her second-floor
>window as the music begins)*

MRS. KRUMP *(Raspy, urban voice)*
Hey, Edward . . . Hey, Edward . . . ! Hey, Edward . . .

come on down here and get your fa'tha! Hey, Edward . . .

DORIS
Hey, lissen ta that cow yell.

BUNNY
Ain't it a shame, girl?
       (BUNNY *starts off*)

CLIFF *(Disgust)*
God dammit . . . Lou. You always tellin' me to be quiet . . . I don't even make half the noise that some of our *good* neighbors do.

DORIS *(To* BUNNY)
Where ya goin', broad?

LOU *(Sitting beside* CLIFF)
Awww . . . she should leave Mr. Krump alone. All he's doin' is peein' aside the pole . . . and then he's goin' in and go ta bed.

BUNNY
Up on "The Avenue."

DORIS
Where?

       (EDDIE KRUMP *sticks his head from his upstairs window. He has dirty blond hair and a sharp, red nose. He is about eleven*)

EDDIE
Ohhh, Christ, Ma . . . what'cha want?

BUNNY
"The Avenue," Doris.

MRS. KRUMP *(Furious)*
Don't you Christ me, Edward . . . Come down here right away, young man!

CLIFF *(To* LOU)
I bet he ain't gonna do it.

DORIS
Ain't you gonna see Ray? That's what you come down this way for.

LOU
He might, Cliff. Besides . . . you the one that's always sayin' everybody here on Derby Street only does what they want to do most of the time, anyway.

BUNNY
He's up there on the step . . . he could see me if he wanted . . . C'mon, girl . . . let's split.

(*They exit*)

CLIFF
'Specially mindin' other people's business.

(RAY *sits between* CLIFF *and* LOU, *one step below them*)

LOU
Wasn't that Bunny, Ray?

RAY
Think I should go and help Mr. Krump out, Cliff?

CLIFF
Nawh.

(*Pause*)

LOU
Why, Cliff?

CLIFF
You stay yo' ass here where ya belong, Ray.

LOU
Don't you talk like that, Cliff.

MRS. KRUMP (*To* EDDIE *in window*)
Eddie . . . are you comin' down here?

EDDIE
Nawh.

CLIFF *(Incredulous)*
Did you hear that?

LOU
Remember . . . we mind our own business.

> *(From the upstairs window of the Garrisons'
> house,* MISS MINNY GARRISON *pushes her
> head; she has a bandanna tied about her head,
> and she is a huge black woman)*

MRS. KRUMP *(Starting for her door)*
I'm going to come up there and beat the hell out of
you, Edward.

> *(*EDDIE *ducks his head in the window as his
> mother enters the door below.*
>
> *Sounds of* MRS. KRUMP's *screams, the shouts
> of* EDDIE KRUMP *and of running feet.*
>
> *Silence.*
>
> *Rhythm 'n blues and gospel music mingle softly.*
>
> RED *and* BAMA *enter at the corner. They see*
> MR. KRUMP *and nod to each other, then slowly,
> stiff-leggedly, stalk about the streetlamp, tight-
> ening the circle about* MR. KRUMP *on each full
> swing around)*

MISS MINNY
Ray . . . wha don't you help Mr. Krump git home?

> *(*RAY *stands and looks up at her)*

RAY
Yas'sum.

CLIFF *(To* RAY*)*
Wha' . . . you gonna go down there and help? . . .

> *(*Ray *hesitates)*

LOU
Awww, Cliff . . . there ain't no harm in it.

CLIFF
No harm?

LOU
Ray always does it.

CLIFF
Well, it's about time he stopped.

MISS MINNY
Go on, Ray. Go on and git Mr. Krump.

RAY
Yas'sum.
        (He trots to the corner)

CLIFF *(Mimics* RAY *in high falsetto)*
Yas'sum.

LOU *(Angry)*
Stop that, Cliff!

CLIFF
Sheeet!

RED
Hey . . . Ray . . . is this lump ah shit a friend of yours? . . .

RAY
Nawh.

LOU
Why don't you stop that stuff, Cliff? Ain't nothin' bein' hurt because Ray's helpin' out Mr. Krump.

BAMA
Maybe they're related.

RED *(Chuckling)*
Hey, man, cool it. I know Ray don't play that. Do you, Ray?

RAY*(Trying to support* MR. KRUMP)
Nawh, Red. Nawh.

RED *(To* BAMA)
See, Bama, Ray don't play the dozens. You better be careful.

BAMA
Shit.

> (RAY *and* BAMA *exchange stares.* BAMA *is several years older than* RAY)

RED
You seen Bunny and Doris, Ray?

RAY
Yeah . . . they headed for "The Avenue."

CLIFF
Nothin' bein' hurt? Just look at that. Look at that, Lou!

> (RAY *has slung* MR. KRUMP *across his shoulder. He is husky and carries his load well.*
>
> *Standing, shouting)*
> Hey, Ray! Make sure his pants fly is zipped up or you'll be a victim of a horrible calamity!

LOU
You think you so smart, Cliff.

BAMA *(To* RAY)
Tote dat bar', boy . . . lift dat bale.

RED *(Booting* RAY *in the seat of the pants)*
Git along, little doggie.

> (CLIFF *is pleased with himself but starts as* RED *kicks* RAY *and stands, but* LOU *tugs at his trouser leg and he sits back down, chuckling over his wit, though scowling at* RED *and* BAMA *who turn laughing and exit.*
>
> RAY *carries his load to the Krumps' door.* CLIFF *lights a cigarette and takes a drink.* LOU *tries to ignore him.*

MRS. KRUMP, *wearing a perpetual worried expression, at her door)*

MRS. KRUMP
Why, thank you, Ray. Just bring him in here and put him on the couch. Thank you, Ray. That Edward is just . . .

> *(They go in,* MRS. KRUMP *at the rear, peering at* MR. KRUMP's *head that dangles down* RAY's *back)*

CLIFF
That goddamn Miss Minny's always startin' some shit!

LOU
Shusss . . . Cliff. She'll hear you.

CLIFF *(Bitter)*
I don't care if the big sow does. Always pretendin' her ears are filled with nothin' but holy holy *gospel* music . . . when they're nothin' but brimmin' with Derby Street dirt.
> *(Mutters)*
Ole bitch!

LOU *(Uneasy)*
Cliff!

CLIFF *(Looks up at* MISS MINNY)
Always startin' some trouble.

> (MISS MINNY *closes her window. Her light goes off)*

LOU
See, she did hear you!

CLIFF
I don't give a damn . . . who she thinks she is anyway?

LOU
Cliff, you just tryin' to start some trouble with Mr. Garrison. You wouldn't say those things if Homer were home.

CLIFF *(Challenging)*
Wouldn't I?

LOU
No, you wouldn't!

CLIFF
I would do anything I do now if ole four-eyed Homer was sittin' right over there on that step pickin' his big nose.

LOU
He don't pick his nose no more.

CLIFF
How do you know? Is that what Miss Minny told you?

LOU
No, Miss Minny didn't tell me a thing. His sister, Marigold, showed me a picture of him in his sergeant's uniform . . . and I know nobody in the United States Army who makes sergeant still picks their nose.

CLIFF
Sheeet!

 (Silence)

LOU
Cliff?

CLIFF *(Angry)*
Look what you've done to that boy, Lou. Look what you and his mother . . .

LOU *(Angry)*
Now don't you start in talkin' 'bout my dead sister!

CLIFF *(Angrier)*
Shut up!
 (Pause and stare)
Don't you see what all of you are tryin' to do . . . Miss Minny . . .

LOU
Who's tryin' to do what, Cliff?

CLIFF *(Continues)*
Miss Minny . . . you . . . all the so-called high-falutin'
pussy on this block . . .

LOU *(Indignant)*
Now you watch your mouth . . .

CLIFF
Pussy! Cunt! Bitches! Always startin' some trouble.

LOU *(Apologetic)*
That was no trouble, Cliff.

CLIFF
It was so . . . Who the hell Miss Minny thinks she is
anyway tellin' Ray to go down there an' get ole man
Krump? And gettin' kicked by that punk Red . . . Ray's
nearly a man . . . he shouldn't . . .

LOU *(Cutting)*
She didn't mean nothin' by it.

CLIFF
Just like she didn't mean nothin' the time she passed
around that petition to have us run off'a Derby Street
when we first moved here.

LOU
She didn't know us then . . . we was strangers. Why
don't you forget it?

CLIFF *(Raising voice)*
What's so strange about us, huh? What was so strange
about us back then when we moved in? What was so
strange? Was we strange because I was goin' ta school
on the G.I. Bill and not tot'in a lunch pail like all
these other asses? . . .

LOU
Shusss . . . Cliff.

CLIFF
I will not shusss . . . that's what they are, aren't they?
Asses! Mules! Donkeys!

LOU
I'm goin' in if you keep that up, Cliff.

THE RADIO
. . . and Fat Abe . . . your local honest used car dealer
is now offering a custom bargain fo' one of you real
swingers out there . . .

(CLIFF *reaches up and pulls the door shut with
a slam, muffling the radio*)

CLIFF
You ain't goin' nowhere just because you don't want to
hear the truth.

(*Silence.* LOU *sulks*)

Well, they are asses . . .
(*Ridicule*)
Derby Street Donkeys!

LOU (*Apologetic*)
Well, I was workin', Cliff. And . . .

CLIFF (*Cutting*)
And they made a hell of a noise about that, too. Always
whisperin' how you work so hard all day in a laundry
for no count me who goes around carryin' books. And
gets home in the middle of the afternoon and jest lays
around like a playboy . . .

LOU
They did see you with them girls all the time, Cliff.

CLIFF
I ain't been with no bitches.

LOU
Cliff . . .

CLIFF
They're lies! That's all . . . every one a lie . . . and don't
you let me hear you tell me them lies again.

(*Silence*)

LOU
Never?

CLIFF
Never!

LOU
What should I say when I find lipstick on your shirt
. . . shades I don't use.

(Silence)

What should I say when I see you flirtin' with the
young girls on the street and with my friends?

(Silence)

CLIFF (Tired)
Light me a cigarette, will ya?

(She does)

LOU
This street ain't so bad now.

CLIFF
Was we so strange because your nephew Ray stays
with us . . . and don't have to work
    (Bitter)
like an ass or mule or fool . . . like a Derby Street
Donkey!

LOU
Cliff!

CLIFF
Why was we so strange?

LOU
Nawh, we wasn't . . .

CLIFF
Who wasn't?

LOU
We wasn't!

CLIFF
Yes, we was!

LOU
Nawh . . . we seemed strange because we always
drinkin' this . . .
> (Raising her glass)

CLIFF
Everybody else drinks somethin' around here . . . ole
man Garrison puts at least a pint of white lightnin'
away a night . . . pure'dee cooked corn whisky!

LOU
But their ignorant oil don't make them yell and hollar
half the night like this wine makes us.

CLIFF (Yells)
Who yells!

LOU (Amused)
. . . and we sing and laugh and you cuss like a sailor.

CLIFF
Who sings and laughs? . . .

LOU
We do!

CLIFF
You a liar!

LOU
Nawh, I'm not, Cliff.
> (He grabs her arm and twists it behind her
> back)

CLIFF
Say you a liar.

LOU
Nawh, Cliff . . . don't do that.

CLIFF (Twists it more)
Who's a liar?

LOU
I am, Cliff.

CLIFF *(A slight jerk)*
Who?

LOU
I am, Cliff. I am!

> *(He releases her)*

CLIFF
That's right . . . sing out when I want you to. Ha ha ha . . .
> *(He tries to caress her)*

LOU *(Rubs arm and shoves him)*
Leave me alone.

CLIFF *(Kisses her)*
I'm glad you finally confessed . . . It'll do your soul some good.

LOU *(Sulking)*
You shouldn't do that, Cliff.

CLIFF
Do what?

LOU
You know what.

CLIFF
Give you spiritual comfort? . . . Apply some soul ointment?

LOU *(Disgusted)*
Awwww . . .

CLIFF
I don't know if you never tell me, hon.

LOU
You know alright.

CLIFF
That I cuss like a sailor?

LOU *(Remembering)*
That's right . . . and . . .

CLIFF *(Cutting)*
Well, you didn't say that.

LOU
I didn't?
        (Pause)
I did too, Cliff.

CLIFF
What?

LOU
Say that we yell and hollar and sing and laugh and cuss like sailors half the night.

CLIFF *(Toasts her)*
Ohhh, Lou. To Lou Lou, my Hottentot queen.

LOU
I'm not!

CLIFF
My queen?

LOU
Hottentot! . . . My features are more northern . . . more Ethiopian.

CLIFF *(Ridicule)*
Haaaah!
        (Pause)
Haaaaah! More northern . . . more Ethiopian! That beak nose of yours comes from that shanty Irishman who screwed your grandmammy down on the plantation.

LOU
Watch your mouth, Cliff.

CLIFF
Watch my mouth?

LOU
Yeah, watch your mouth. Some things I just won't allow you to say.

CLIFF *(Mocking)*
"Some things I just won't allow you to say."
  (Offended)
Watch my mouth? Well, take a look at yours. Yours comes from that Ubangi great granddaddy on your father's side . . . your "northern" nose, well, we've gone through its . . .

LOU *(Warning)*
Stop it, Cliff!

CLIFF
. . . but your build is pure Hottentot, darling . . . and that's why I shall forever love you . . . however the Derby Street Donkeys bray about me being with other girls . . . younger, prettier girls, mind you . . . But Lou, baby, you are married to an "A" number one ass man . . . and *yours* is one of the Hottentot greats of northern America.

LOU *(Indignant)*
Fuck you!

CLIFF *(Fake dialect)*
Wahl, hon-nee chile . . . I just wanted ta tell yawhl dat yo' husband is one ob dem connoisseurs of dem fleshy Hottentot parts which'n yous is so wonderfully invested wit'.

LOU
Fuck you, Cliff! . . . Ohhh, just listen to that. You make me say bad things, man. You think you so smart and know all them big words since you been goin' to school. You still ain't nothin' but a lowdown bastard at heart as far as I'm concerned.

  (Silence.

CLIFF *takes a drink.* LOU *is wary but defiant)*

CLIFF *(Smiles)*
We do cuss too much, don't we?

LOU *(Smiles)*
And we drink too much.

> *(He pulls her over and fondles her; she kisses
> him but pushes him away)*

CLIFF
Like sailors?

LOU
Yes!

CLIFF *(Amused)*
I thought we cussed like sailors.

LOU
We do.

CLIFF *(Raises voice)*
Make up yo' mind, broad. Now what is it . . . do we
cuss and drink like sailors or cuss like sailors and
drink like . . . like . . . like . . . what?

LOU
Like niggers.

> *(At the last word lights go up on other stoops,
> revealing the occupants looking at* CLIFF *and*
> LOU.
>
> *Then lights dim and come up on "The Avenue."
> The figures of* RED, BAMA, DORIS *and*
> BUNNY GILLETTE *are seen)*

BUNNY GILLETTE
Go on now, Red . . . stop messin' with me.

RED
Awww . . . woman . . . stop all your bullshit. You know
you like me to feel your little ass . . . c'mere.

DORIS
Stop fucken with that girl, Red.

RED
What's wrong, Doris? You jealous or somethin'?

DORIS
Man . . . if you melted and turned to water and ran down the gutter I wouldn't even step over you.

RED
Why . . . scared I'd look up your dress and see your tonsils?

BUNNY GILLETTE *(Giggling)*
Ohhh . . . girl, ain't he bad.

BAMA
C'mere, Doris. I wanna talk to you.

DORIS
You ain't never wanted to talk to me before, Bama.

> (RED *has his arm about* BUNNY GILLETTE's *waist.* BAMA *takes* DORIS's *hand)*

RED
C'mon, Bunny . . . I'll buy you a fish sandwich.
(To BAMA)
Hey, Bam ah lam . . . do you think these broads deserve a fish sandwich?

BAMA
Nawh, man, they don't deserve shit.

DORIS
Hey, Bunny, we really hooked us some sports . . . you better make it back to Ray, girl.

> *(Lights down on "The Avenue."*
>
> *Lights up on Derby Street.* CLIFF *and* LOU *laugh as* RAY *comes out of the Krumps'. The radio is muffled in the background)*

MRS. KRUMP *(Off)*
You sure you don't want another slice of cake and a glass of milk, Raymond?

RAY
Nawh, thank you, Mrs. Krump.

> (EDDIE KRUMP *sticks his head out of his window*)

EDDIE
Thanks ah lot, Ray.

RAY
That's okay; why don't you come on down for a while?

EDDIE
Nawh . . . I can't . . . I gotta headache.

CLIFF *(To* RAY)
Little white Eddie don't want to come down after you carry his pissy pukey drunk daddy in for him, huh?

LOU
Cliff!

RAY *(Embarrassed)*
Nawh.

LOU
Cliff . . . no wonder they sent around that petition. Just look how you act.

CLIFF *(Angry)*
Yeah, just look how I act . . . fuck how I act!

LOU
You got the dirtiest mouth, Cliff.

CLIFF *(Angrier)*
Fuck how I act . . . fuck it!
> (CLIFF *stands and glares about at his neighbors. They turn their heads and resume their activities*)

LOU
Just like a sailor.

CLIFF *(Satisfied)*
Yup . . . just like I always said . . . folks on Derby Street sure know how to mind their own business.

LOU
Just like the no-'count sailor I met and married.

CLIFF
Well, I am a mathafukken shit-ass sailor. The same you met and married, Lou.

LOU
Not any more.

CLIFF
Still! I still am. Once a sailor . . . always a sailor.

LOU
Not any more. Besides . . . you stayed most of your time in the guardhouse.

CLIFF *(To* RAY)
Listen to that . . . listen to that, Ray. Guardhouse.

LOU
That was the reason I married you. Felt sorry for you and knew your commanding officer would go light on you if he knew you had been married when you deserted and not put you in the guardhouse for so long.

CLIFF
Yeah?

LOU
Yeah!

CLIFF
Don't think you did me any favors, baby.

LOU
Well, who else did? I went to your ship and testified . . . I kept you from gettin' a bad discharge. In fact,

I'm the one who made a man out of you even though
your mother and the whole entire United States Navy
failed.

CLIFF *(Mutters)*
Bitch!

LOU
Do you hear that? Failed . . . to make a man or a
sailor of ya.

CLIFF *(Ridicule)*
Ray. This broad, pardon the expression, this woman
named Lou . . . Lou Ellen Margarita Crawford Dawson
. . . who calls herself your aunt, by the way . . .

LOU
I am his aunt!

CLIFF
This bitch don't know what a sailor is.

LOU
I don't? . . . I don't? Then I guess you know even
though you spent most of your navy time in the guardhouse.

RAY
Brig, Lou . . .

CLIFF
Thank you, son. Thank you.

LOU
What? . . .

RAY
Brig, Lou . . . not guardhouse.

CLIFF
That's right . . . that's fucken "A" right . . .

LOU *(Mutters and takes a drink)*
Dirtiest mouth I ever heard.

CLIFF
That's a lie . . . your sister has the dirtiest mouth in north, south, west and all of this town.
(To RAY)
That's your play-aunt Doris I'm talkin' about, Ray, not your dear dead mother . . . may she rest in peace . . .

LOU
You two-faced bastard. Listen to you soundin' like one of them white missionaries . . . "May she rest in peace . . ." Dirty-mouthed liar!

CLIFF
Liar? About what? My not being in the guardhouse?

RAY
Brig.

LOU
You know that's not what I mean.

CLIFF
Pour yourself a drink, Ray. Put some hair on your . . . ding-a-ling.
(Begins humming)

LOU
I pity the day you talked me into allowing Ray to take a drink.

CLIFF
Whatta ya mean? He was a lush when he came here. His mother and him both almost drank themselves to death.

LOU
Cliff!

CLIFF *(Defensive)*
Ain't that right, Ray?

RAY
Sort'a. I did kinda drink along with Mamma for a while until they put her away.

CLIFF

Sort'a? Stop jivin' . . . for a youngblood you can really hide some port.

RAY *(Flattered)*

Yeah . . . I do my share.

LOU

Now, Ray, I want you to . . .

CLIFF *(Loud)*

Quiet! You heard him . . . he does his share. Here's a toast to you, youngblood.
        (Lifts his glass)
To Ray who does his share.

        (They drink, except for LOU)

RAY

Thanks, Cliff.

CLIFF

Don't mention it, Ray. Just don't mention it at all. It's your world, son. It's really your world.
        (To LOU)
Well, isn't it?

        (Silence)

You don't feel like toasting Ray?

        (Silence)

Ray . . . you know, Lou is a lot like your mother used to be. Quiet, except that your mother usually had a glass up to her mouth instead of her mouth clamped tight.

LOU

You shouldn't of said that, Cliff. You're goin'a pay for that.

CLIFF

Pay? Ray, it's your world . . . does your ole Uncle Cliff have to pay?

IN THE WINE TIME 129

RAY
Well, I don't . . .

LOU *(Cutting)*
Stop it, Cliff. Ray, I'm sorry. Cliff gets too much to drink in him . . .

CLIFF *(Loud, cutting)*
Nice night we havin' out here on our white well-scrubbed steps . . .

(Both together)

LOU	CLIFF
. . . and he runs off at the mouth somethin' terrible. I know you wasn't much past twelve when I came an' got you and kept them from puttin' you in a home. And you had already started in drinkin' 'n smokin' and foolin' around with girls . . . and I knew you drank too much for a growin' boy, much less a man. But I couldn't see you in a home—it would have messed you up . . . or sent down South to Cousin Frank's. I don't mean you so young you don't know what you want to do, Ray. I'm only six years older than you . . . but Cliff still shouldn't be givin' you so much wine and teachin' you bad habits.	. . . with all of God's white stars shinin' above your black heads. Ain't that right, Lord? You old shyster. You pour white heat on these niggers, these Derby Street Donkeys, in the daytime and roast and fry them while they shovel shit for nex' to nothin', and steam them at night like big black lobsters . . . ha ha . . . the Krumps are little red lobsters of Yourn . . . and they just drink, an' screw in the dark, and listen to jive talk an' jive music an' jive *holy* music . . . but they still think they have to face You in the mornin'. That's right, face You, You jive-ass sucker! They don't know they

It ain't good for none of us, not even me. I hardly know where I'm at some of the times when I start in drinkin' after I come from work ... but it sho' do relaxes me. And your mother is gonna call me to account for it when we meet up in heaven ... I really know that. The devil's in Cliff, I know that, to do what he's doin' to us ... and I ain't helpin' things much. Listen to what I say, Ray, and not to the devil. Listen to me, Ray. got to face Your jive-hot, blazin' face ... simple niggers ... but they do 'cause they believe in You and Your lies. Stupid donkeys! They only got to look my god in the face once and forget about You, You jive-time sucker ...

> *(Remembering an old joke)*

... ha ha ... she's black as night and as cool and slick as a king snake ...

> *(Singing)*

... Yes, Lord, yes, Lord, yes, Lord, yes, Lord ...

LOU
Stop it, Cliff! You're drunk 'n' crazy 'n' drivin' me out of my head!

> *(Silence.* CLIFF *stares at her)*

RAY *(To both)*
It's all right. It's all right.

LOU
Ray, when I get to heaven your mother's gonna have a lot to say to me.

CLIFF *(Laughs)*
Heaven?

LOU
Yeah, heaven. And you better get some of the fear of the Lord in you, Cliff.

CLIFF *(Disgust)*
Every night. Every goddamn night when you start in feelin' your juice.

LOU
'Cause I know better, that's why.

CLIFF
Is that why when I get you in bed every night you
hollar:
    (Whining falsetto)
"Yes, Lord. Yes, Lord. Ohhh . . . Jesus . . . one more
time."

    (RAY *giggles*)

LOU
You're bad, Cliff. You're bad. Bad!

CLIFF
Sho' I'm bad, hon-nee chile.
    (Singing)
I'm forty hands across mah chest . . . don't fear nothin'
. . . not God nor death . . . I got a tombstone mind
an' a graveyard disposition . . . I'm a bad mathafukker
an' I don't mind . . . dyin'.

LOU *(Cutting)*
You're just a dirty-mouthed . . .

CLIFF *(Cutting)*
Yeah, I know . . . and I'll have you know that just
because I spent one third of my navy time in various
brigs, not just one, understand, baby girl, but at least
an even dozen between here and Istanbul, that I was
still one of the saltiest salt water sailors in the fleet
. . . on dry land, in the fleet or in some fucken marine
brig!

LOU
You wasn't shit, Cliff . . . You know that, don't you?

CLIFF
Sticks 'n' stones, Lou . . . sticks 'n' stones.

LOU
Pour me a drink, Ray . . . and give your no-'count step-
uncle one too.

(RAY *pours drinks for the three of them*)

CLIFF
Step-uncle? Now how in Jesus' name did I get demoted from uncle to step?

LOU
You just did . . . suddenly you just stepped down.

RAY
Do you think I can get into the navy, Cliff?

CLIFF *(Grabs* LOU's *arm)*
Sometimes, Lou . . .

RAY
Huh, Cliff?

CLIFF *(Recovering)*
Navy? . . . Why sure . . . sure, Ray. When you come of age I'll sign the papers myself.

LOU
Steps can't, Cliff. But I can.

CLIFF
I can, Lou . . . I should know.
      (Proudly)
I joined on my sixteenth birthday.

LOU
Steps can't.

CLIFF *(Pinches her shoulder)*
Bitch!

LOU *(Feigning)*
Owww, Cliff. Owww.

RAY
If I'm of age than you won't have to sign, will ya?

CLIFF
No, I won't. Not if you're of age, Ray.

LOU
He can't sign anyway.

CLIFF
I can too, Ray. You just watch me when the time comes.

RAY
I'll be sixteen next week, Cliff.

CLIFF
You will?

RAY
Yeah.

CLIFF
Already?

RAY
Yeah.

CLIFF *(To* LOU)
He will?

LOU
If that's what he says.

CLIFF
Damn . . . so soon.

LOU
Sixteen ain't old enough. You have to be seventeen before they'll even let me sign for you, Ray.

CLIFF
I went when I was sixteen . . . my sixteenth birthday.

LOU *(Peeved)*
That's because you were down in Virginia in the woods . . . fool! They don't even have birth certificates down there . . . you could of went when you were thirteen if your mother had'a sworn you was old enough.

CLIFF
I was too old enough!

LOU
No, you wasn't. And Ray ain't either. He's got to wait until he's seventeen. And then I might sign for him.

RAY
I got to wait? But Uncle Cliff said I could go.

CLIFF
Yeah, you can go, Ray. I'll sign the papers myself. You're goin' to the navy and see how real men live.

LOU *(Angry)*
He's not goin' . . . he's not old enough . . . and you ain't signin' no papers for him, Cliff. His mother wouldn't . . .

CLIFF
I'll sign anything I want fo' him. I'm his guardian . . .

LOU *(Ridicule)*
Guardian? How? With what? You ain't never had a job in your life over six months. What you raise him with . . . the few lousy bucks you don't drink up from your government check? You somebody's guardian . . . I . . .

(CLIFF *slaps her violently*)

CLIFF *(Low, menacing)*
You talk too much, Lou.

LOU *(Defiant)*
It's my responsibility, Cliff. Mine. Mine. My responsibility. I'm not going to sign or let you sign. His mother . . .

CLIFF
Damn that! Damn it! I don't care what his dead mother wants. Who the hell cares what the dead want? It's what Ray wants that counts. He's got to get out of here . . . don't you, Ray? . . . Off'a Derby Street and away from here so he can grow up to be his own man.

LOU *(Crying)*
Like you?

CLIFF
No, not like me . . . not tied down to a half-grown, scared, childish bitch!

LOU
You don't have to be.

CLIFF
But I love you.

>*(Lights down, up on "The Avenue."*

>RED *slaps* BUNNY GILLETTE)

DORIS
Red . . . you mathafukker . . . Stop that!

BUNNY GILLETTE *(Crying)*
Go on now, Red. Leave me alone . . .

RED
Bitch! Who you think you tellin' to kiss your ass? You want me to kiss your nasty ass?

BAMA *(Reaching for him)*
Hey, lighten up, Red.

DORIS
Leave her alone!

RED *(Being held by* BAMA)
You want me to kiss your . . .

BUNNY GILLETTE
Nawh, Red. Nawh.

DORIS *(A short knife in her hand)*
You better not touch her again . . . you better not. You goin'a be sorry for this.

>*(Lights down on "The Avenue" and up on Derby Street)*

RAY
I'm sorry, Lou.

LOU
It's alright, Ray. We've fought before . . . I'm just
sorry you have to see us act like this.

CLIFF
Awww, honey . . . I'll forget it if you do.

LOU
You beat on me and I'm supposed to forget it? In my
condition.

CLIFF
You got nearly six months before the baby. He can't
get hurt by just a little . . .

LOU
You know the doctor told you not to be hittin' on me
no mo'. You did it on purpose 'cause you don't want it.

CLIFF
I'm sorry, Lou.

LOU
It's a wonder you didn't hit me in the stomach.

CLIFF
Well, it's a wonder I didn't.

LOU
See there. You don't want it.

CLIFF
Nawh, I don't want a baby I can't take care of . . . do
you?

LOU
You can get a job.

CLIFF
At a dollar an hour? Dollar-an-hour Dawson, that's
me. Nawh, I don't want any kids until I can afford
them. That's why I'm goin' ta school.

LOU
You studying business so you can take care of me an'

IN THE WINE TIME

your kids? What kind of job can you get in business? You got money to open you a business?

CLIFF
Lou, we've gone over this before. I'll manage.

LOU
Like you have gettin' a job?

CLIFF
Well, you want me to get a job in the laundry? Like all your cousins?

LOU
And me!

CLIFF
Startin' at a buck an hour. Hell no, I won't work!

LOU *(Scared)*
But what are we goin'a do when your checks run out, Cliff?

CLIFF
Me? I'll do the best I can. Maybe ship out again.

LOU
No, Cliff!

CLIFF
If I can't turn up anything . . . well, you and the kid can get on relief.

(Silence)

LOU
Where's your pride? A big strong man like . . .

CLIFF
A dollar an hour don't buy that much pride, Lou. There's a big rich world out there . . . I'm goin'a get me part of it or not at all.

(Both together)

LOU
You ain't no man. My daddy he worked twenty years with his hands ... his poor hands are hard and rough with corns and callouses. He was a man ... he worked and brought us up to take pride in ourselves and to fear God. What did I marry? I thought you was a man, Cliff. I thought because you was loud and was always fightin' and drinkin' and was so big and strong that you was a man ... but you ain't nothin' but a lowdown and less than nothin'!

CLIFF
I'm goin' ta get me part of that world or stare your God in the eye and scream *why*. I am not a beast ... an animal to be used for the plows of the world. But if I am then I'll act like one, I'll be one and turn this fucken world of dreams and lies and fairy tales into a jungle or a desert. And I don't give much of a happy fuck which. There's a world out there, woman. Just beyond that lamppost ... just across "The Avenue" and it'll be mine and Ray's.

LOU *(Screams)*
You're nothin'!

CLIFF
In the navy Ray can travel and see things and learn and meet lots of different ...

LOU
No ! ! !

CLIFF
... girls and make somethin' ...

LOU
Is that what it did for you?

CLIFF
Yeah, that's what it did for me!

LOU

Well, I don't want him to be like you.

CLIFF

How would you want him to be like . . . one of the Derby Street Donkeys? Or one of the ditty boppers or an avenue hype . . . or . . . a drug addict . . . or what?

LOU *(Standing)*

He ain't turned out so bad so far.
>   *(Determined)*
He's not goin', Cliff.
>   *(Pause)*
Ray, just get it out of your mind. I'm not signin' no navy papers . . . you're too young.
>   *(She enters the house as the lights fade to black-ness)*

CURTAIN

ACT II

Mythic blues plays. Lights up on "The Avenue."

The couples are in embrace.

BUNNY GILLETTE *(To* RED)
I like you a lot . . . really I do . . . but what will Ray say?

RED
Fuck that little punk!

DORIS *(To* RED)
What you say 'bout my nephew?

BAMA
He wasn't talkin' to you, Doris.

BUNNY GILLETTE
You ain't gonna fight me anymo' . . . are ya, Red?

DORIS
I'd cut that nigger's nut off if he had'a hit me like that, Bunny!

BAMA
You wouldn'a do nothin', Doris . . . you just . . .

DORIS
Yeah, I would . . . and that goes double for any jive nigger who lays a finger on me or mine!

RED *(Places his hands on* BUNNY's *rear)*
Why don't all you mathafukkers shut up! Can't you see I'm concentratin'?

> *(Lights down, up on Derby Street.*
>
> CLIFF *and* RAY *sit upon their stoop. The remainder of the street is in shadow.*

Silence.

From the last stoop up the street BEATRICE *detaches herself from the shadows and walks toward the corner.*

She is a buxom, brown girl and carries herself proudly. She speaks as she passes each shadowy group of forms upon the stoops)

THE RADIO
It's seventy-eight degrees . . . that's seven . . . eight . . .

BEATRICE *(Passing)*
Hello, Mr. Cooper. Miz Cooper.

SHADOWS
Hello, Beatrice. How you doin' tonight?

BEATRICE *(Passing)*
Hello, Miss Francis.

SHADOWS
Why hello, Bea. How ya doin', girl?

BEATRICE *(Passing)*
Hello, Mr. Roy.

SHADOWS
Howdy, Beatrice. How's your folks?

BEATRICE
Just fine.
> *(She passes on.*

> MISS MINNY *puts her head out her window.* BEATRICE *passes* CLIFF *and* RAY *without speaking, her pug nose up, her head sighting on something upon the Derby Street fence, on the far side of the street.*

> BEATRICE *comes abreast the Garrisons' house and looks up)*
Hello, Miss Minny.

MISS MINNY
Hello, Beatrice . . . how y'all?

BEATRICE *(Stops)*
Just fine, Miss Minny. How's Marigold and Ruth?

MISS MINNY
Awww . . . they're fine, Beatrice. They off visitin' mah sister this week.

BEATRICE
That's nice, Miss Minny. Tell them I asked about them, will ya?

MISS MINNY
All right, dear. Did you know that Homer asked about you in his last letter?

BEATRICE
No, I didn't. Is he still in Korea?

MISS MINNY
Yeah, he's still over there. They done made him a sergeant.

BEATRICE
Yes, I know. Marigold told me. He's doing okay, isn't he?

MISS MINNY
Oh, yes, he's just doin' fine and everything. Says he likes it over there.

BEATRICE
Tell him I asked about him, will you?

MISS MINNY
All right, Beatrice.

> (BEATRICE *continues, and reaching the corner, she exits.* MISS MINNY *withdraws and shuts her window)*

THE RADIO
. . . And now the genius of the great . . .

> *(Music plays, softly)*

CLIFF
Sheeet.

RAY
What'cha say, Cliff?

(*Silence.*

Both together)

CLIFF	RAY
I said that ...	I wonder if ...

(*Silence.*

Both together)

(*Annoyed*)	(*Embarrassed*)
Go on!	Excuse me.

(*Lengthy silence. Both take drinks and drag
upon their cigarettes*)

CLIFF (*Hurriedly*)
How old's that broad?

RAY
How old? ...

CLIFF
Yeah.

RAY
Oh, Bea? ... About my age, I guess.

CLIFF
She's certainly a snotty little stuckup heifer, ain't she?

RAY
Yeah, I guess so.

(*Silence.*

Both together)

CLIFF (*Almost leering*)	RAY (*Explaining*)
I wonder what ...	She's always ...

(*Both halt. CLIFF stubs out his cigarette*)

CLIFF *(Yells over his shoulder)*
Hey, Lou!

>*(No answer.*
>
>*To* RAY)

Guess she's out back in the kitchen or the john.

RAY
Yeah.

CLIFF
Ray?

RAY
Huh?

CLIFF
Did you ever get any ah that?

RAY
Beatrice?

CLIFF
Yeah.

RAY
Nawh.

CLIFF
What she doin', savin' it for Homer?

RAY
Homer?
>*(Laughing)*

She can't stand Homer. Calls him "Ole Country."

CLIFF
What'cha waitin' on, boy?

RAY
Nothin'.

CLIFF
When I was yo' age I'd ah had every little pussy on Derby Street all to myself.

RAY
You'd have them all sewed up, huh?

CLIFF *(Not perceiving* RAY's *humor)*
Yeah, sho' would.

RAY
Ahhhuh.

CLIFF
How "bout Marigold and Ruth?

RAY
What about them?

CLIFF
You ain't gettin' none of that either?

RAY
Nawh.

CLIFF
Why not, boy? What's the matter with you?

RAY
Nothin'.

CLIFF
Nothing?

RAY
Nawh, nothin'.

CLIFF
With all this good stuff runnin' 'round here you lettin'
the chance of a lifetime slip by . . .

RAY
Yeah, I guess I am.

CLIFF
. . . always over there on Thirteenth Street messin'
round with li'l Bunny when you should be takin' care
of business back home.

RAY
I don't like any of the girls round here.

CLIFF
What's wrong with them? A girl's a girl ... well, most
of them are anyway.

RAY *(Embarrassed)*
Well, I like Bunny. Me and her's in love.

CLIFF
In love? In love?
     (Cracking the door and over the music)
Hey, Lou Ellen ... Your nephew's in love!

     (No answer.

     Muttering)
Must'a fell in.
     (Looking at RAY*)*
Boy ... you got a lot to learn.

RAY
I can't help it, Cliff. And she loves me too.

CLIFF
Ohhh, yeah ... you really got a lot to learn.

RAY
Cliff ... I ...

CLIFF
Just because she comes down here with you on the
nights that me and Lou are out don't make you be in
love. You didn't think I knew, huh? Well, who the hell
you think been turnin' those pillows on the couch over
an' wipin' them off? Not your Aunt Lou ... nawh
nawh, she'd damn near die if she knew you were doin'
what comes naturally.

RAY
I'm sorry, Cliff.

CLIFF
Forget it. Oh yeah, now that reminds me. Clean up
your own mess from now on. You're big enough.

RAY
Okay.

CLIFF
Bunny's the first girl you've had?

RAY
Nawh.

CLIFF
How many?

RAY
'Bout half a dozen.

(Silence)

CLIFF
Well . . . you ain't exactly backward . . . but still when
I was your age . . . but let's forget about that.

RAY
Okay.

CLIFF
Now what about Marigold and Ruth, don't they like
you?

RAY
All the girls on the street like me, I guess . . . 'cept'n
Beatrice 'n' she used to let me kiss her . . .

CLIFF
She did, huh? Well, what happened?

RAY
I don't know.

CLIFF
Well, why don't you get one of the girls next door?
Screw one of Homer's sisters.
(Chuckling)
Get some of his stuff while he's away.

RAY
Yeah . . . yeah, Marigold likes me a lot. Homer even
wants me to get Marigold so I might have to marry
her and he'd have a brother-in-law he'd like, but she

don't want it, not like that, and I don't see the sense of goin' with a girl if I can't do it to her.

CLIFF
You showin' some sense there, Ray. An' forget about that marriage stuff too.

RAY
Yeah, and Ruth wants to get married too bad. I'm scared as hell of her.

(Silence)

CLIFF
Yeah, you better stick with fast little Bunny. Gettin' you in the service is gonna be hard enough . . . If your aunt knew that anyone was thinkin' about you and marriage . . . we'd really have a case on our hands. She'd probably lock you up in the cellar.

RAY (Contemplating)
And Beatrice thinks she's better than anybody else.

CLIFF
Yeah. I guess you do know what you're doin' stickin' with Bunny. But you'll be gone in a month anyway.

RAY
In a week.

CLIFF
Yeah, that's right . . . in a week . . . And things will be different then for you.
(Pause)
Hey, do you know what, Ray?

RAY (Slowly)
I met a girl the other day.

CLIFF
Do you know what, Ray?

RAY
I met a girl the other day, Cliff.

CLIFF
You did?

RAY *(More sure)*
Yeah, I met her the other day . . . she's almost a
woman.

CLIFF
She is?

RAY
A pretty girl.

CLIFF
You met her where, Ray?

> *(Lights down, and up on "The Avenue."*
>
> *The* GIRL *appears and stands under soft light.
> She has huge eyes and her skin is a soft black.*
>
> *The couples are fixed in tableau but* RED *and*
> BAMA *pull away from* BUNNY GILLETTE
> *and* DORIS *and dance about the* GIRL *in a se-
> duction dance, until the two girls break their
> position and dance against the attraction of the
> girl, in a symbolic castration of the boys.*
>
> *Lights down to fantasy hues on "The Avenue"
> and up on* CLIFF *and* RAY)

RAY
I met her over on "The Avenue."

CLIFF
Yeah, and she was pretty?

RAY
Yeah.

CLIFF
That's good. But you better not get stuck on her.

RAY
Why? Why, Cliff?

CLIFF
'Cause you goin' away in a month. You goin' to the navy, remember?

RAY
But she can wait for me.

CLIFF
Well . . . most women are funny. They don't wait around too long. They get anxious . . . you know, nervous that they won't get something that they think belongs to them. Never could understand what that somethin' was, but most of them are on the lookout for it, whinin' for it all the time, demandin' it. And I guess some of them even get it.

RAY
She'll wait.

CLIFF
Don't be too sure, son. Most of them don't.

RAY
Lou waited for you, didn't she?

(Silence)

Didn't she?

(Silence)

CLIFF
Yeah . . . but that was a little different.

RAY
How?

CLIFF
It was just different . . . that's all.

RAY
But how would it be different for you and Lou and not for me and my girl?

CLIFF
Well, for one, I don't know your girl so I can't say

positively just how she'd act . . . And, two, and you better not breathe a word of this to your aunt . . . you hear?

>   *(Pause)*

Well, Lou Ellen is different because . . . well, because she's got character.

RAY
My girl . . .

CLIFF *(Cutting)*
And your aunt's got principle and conviction and you have to be awfully special for that.

RAY
But, Cliff . . .

CLIFF *(Continuing)*
. . . Now don't tell her, your aunt, I said these things, but she's special in that way.

RAY
I won't tell her.

CLIFF
For someone to have all of them qualities in these times is close to bein' insane. She's either got to be hopelessly ignorant or have the faith of an angel . . . and she's neither.

RAY
Nawh, I don't guess she is.

CLIFF
I don't deserve her, I know.

RAY
You two pretty happy together, aren't you?

CLIFF
Ray?

RAY
Yeah.

CLIFF
Don't think about her too much.

RAY
Lou?

CLIFF
Nawh ... you know. Your girl.

RAY
Oh.

CLIFF
Yeah.

RAY *(Distant)*
Yeah, I guess so.

CLIFF
Why do you say it like that?

RAY
Awww, I was just thinkin'. Lou says I can't go ... and ... and this girl ... she ... well, I see her every day now and ...

CLIFF
Have you ...

RAY *(Upset, cutting)*
Nawh! We don't ... we don't need to do anything. We just look at each other and smile ... that's all.

CLIFF
Smile?

RAY
Yeah.

CLIFF
What else?

RAY
That's all. I just wait on the corner for her every afternoon and she comes dancing along with her little

funny walk and sometimes she hums or sings to me a while . . . then smiles some more and goes away . . .

(Lights down on "The Avenue" and the dancers)

CLIFF
Boy, you better git yourself another drink.

RAY
I won't see her no more if I go to the navy, Cliff.

CLIFF
There's other things to see. Get her out of your head, Ray. There's a lot more fish in the ocean . . . ha ha . . . and a lot more girls where she came from. Girls all sizes and shapes . . .

RAY *(Protesting)*
You don't know where she came from!

CLIFF
Why don't I? I just need to take one look at any girl and I know all about her. And with yours . . . well, your just tellin' me about her makes me know. I know all about her, Ray. And let me give you some advice . . . now you trust me, don't you?
(Pause)
Good. I want you to stay away from her. There's all kinds of girls on this stinkin' planet . . . speakin' all kinds of tongues you never would think of, comin' in all kinds of shades and colors and everything. When you become a swabby, the world will open up to you.

Say, maybe you'll go to France . . . to Nice or Marseilles . . . the Riviera. Lie out in the hot sun . . . you won't need a suntan but you can lie out there anyway so those tourists and Frenchmen can see you and envy you. And you'll see all those sexy French broads in their handkerchief bathin' suits. Yeah, I can see you now, Ray, out there in your bright red trunks with sunglasses on peekin' at those girls. Or maybe you'll go to Italy and git you some of that dago stuff. Ha ha ha . . . best damn poon tang in the world, boy.

(He ruffles RAY's woolly head and takes a good-sized drink)
Ha ha ha . . . put hair on your tonsils.
(Pause. Laughing)
Yeah, there's nothin' like walkin' down a street in your navy blues. You know . . . you know . . . you should get tailor-made, skin tights, Ray, with buttons up both sides, and have your wallet slung around back of your pants . . . I can see you now. Your wallet will be fat as a Bible. And . . . and the pretty little broads will be callin' out to you. "Hey, Yankee! Hey, sailor! Hey, Joe! Fucky fucky . . . two American dollah!" Ha ha ha ha . . . yeah!

Yeah, that's livin', Ray. That's livin'.

RAY *(Enthused)*
Is it, Cliff? Is it?

CLIFF
In some ports you can get a quart of the best imported whisky for two bucks and in some ports you can get the best brandy for only a buck or so.

And the nights . . . ahhh . . . the nights at sea, boy. Ain't nothin' like it. To be on watch on a summer night in the South Atlantic or the Mediterranean when the moon is full is enough to give a year of your life for, Ray. The moon comes from away off and is all silvery, slidin' across the rollin' ocean like a path of cold, wet white fire, straight into your eye. Nothin' like it. Nothin' like it to be at sea . . . unless it's to be in port with a good broad and some mellow booze.

RAY
Do you think I can get in, Cliff?

CLIFF
Sure you can. Sure. Don't worry none about what your Aunt Lou says . . . I've got her number. I'll fix it up.

RAY
I sure hope you can.

CLIFF
Sure I can. As long as I tell your aunt I'm fixin' to ship out she'll sell you, herself, and probably her soul to keep me with her.

RAY *(Frowning)*
You goin'a ship out, Cliff?

CLIFF
Nawh . . . nawh . . . I had my crack at the world . . . and I've made it worse, if anything . . . you young-bloods own the future . . . remember that . . . I had my chance. All I can do now is sit back and raise fat babies. It's your world now, boy.

> *(TINY rounds the corner)*

Well, here comes Tiny.
> *(Knocks on door behind him with his elbow)*
Lou. Lou. Here comes little Tiny.

> *(It has gotten darker and the shadowy figures have disappeared from the other stoops, into the doors of the houses, one after another)*

LOU *(Off)*
What'cha want, Cliff? I just washed my hair.

CLIFF
It's Tiny . . . she's comin' down the street.

> *(TINY is a small, attractive girl in her late teens. As she comes abreast of the alley a large man in wide-brimmed hat jumps out at her and shouts)*

CLARK
Boo!

TINY
Aaaaaiieeeeeee ! ! !

> *(After the scream there is recognition between the two and CLARK laughs, nearly hysterically, and begins trotting first in a circle about TINY,*

*who looks furious enough to cry, then across the
street to the fence where he leans and laughs,
pounding the boards with his fists.*

Windows go up)

MRS. KRUMP
Is anything wrong?

MISS MINNY
What's all dat noise out dere?

LOU *(At door, her hair disheveled)*
Clark, you shouldn't go 'round scarin' people like that!

    (The POLICEMAN *passes the corner and stops
and looks over the scene)*

TINY *(Regains breath)*
You ole stupid mathafukker!

MRS. KRUMP
Is anyone hurt?

CLIFF *(Stands, his arm around* TINY's *shoulder)*
Nawh, Krumpy . . . the goddamn natives are restless,
that's all.

MRS. KRUMP
Ohhhh . . . I'm sorry . . . I just wanted to help.
    (Her window closes)

MISS MINNY
You and your friends shouldn't all the time be usin'
that kinda language, Cliff . . . gives the street a bad
name. We got enough bad streets and boys around
here without you makin' it worse.

CLIFF
If you kept your head in where it belongs you wouldn't
hear so much, Miss Minny. Now would you?

MISS MINNY
I'm gonna talk to somebody 'bout you, Cliff. Somethin'
should be done about you.
    (Her window closes)

THE POLICEMAN
Is everything okay, Cliff?

CLIFF
Yeah, Officer Murphy. Everything's great.

THE POLICEMAN
Well keep it that way. I want it quiet around here,
Cliff.
        (*The* POLICEMAN *turns the corner*)

RAY
His name's not Murphy, Cliff.

CLIFF
To me it is . . . If he doesn't know to call my right
name I don't know his.

RAY
He said Cliff.

CLIFF
Yeah, he said Cliff like he was sayin' boy. He didn't
say Mr. Dawson.

LOU *(Ridicule)*
Mr. Dawson . . . and his mob.

TINY
I'm sorry, Cliff. I didn't mean to make all that noise
. . . but that stupid ole Clarkie over there . . .

CLIFF
That's okay, Tiny. It's not your fault. Old nose for
news up there has been after us as long as I can remember.
        (*To* CLARK)
Hey, Silly Willy . . . come the hell on over here and
stop tryin' to tear down those people's fence . . . besides, it wasn't that funny anyway.

RAY
You sho' can holler, Tiny.

TINY

I was afraid, man. Some big old stupid thing like that jumps out at you. Damn, man . . . I'm just a little thing . . . he makes two of me.

LOU

From the way you hollar, sister, I know they'll have to want you really bad to get you.

TINY

Fucken "A," baby. If they want mah little ass they gonna have to bring ass.

CLIFF

With Clark's big bad feet he couldn't catch a cold.

TINY

I should'a known better than to be walkin' along beside some alley, anyway. If I hadn't seen you folks up here on the steps I would'a been out in the middle of the street with runnin' 'n' hollarin' room all around.

RAY

You still didn't do so bad.

> (CLARK *comes over, snuffling and wheezing. He has a large moon face and is in his early thirties*)

CLARK *(Giggles)*

I'm sorry, Tiny . . . ha ha ha . . . but I couldn't help myself when I saw you over on Ninth Street turn the corner.

TINY *(Peeved)*

You been following me that long, man?

CLARK *(Nearly convulsed)*

Heee heee . . . yeah, I ran through the alley and waited . . . and . . . heee heee . . . and when . . . heee heee . . . I heard your walk I jumped out.

LOU *(Angry)*

Somebody's goin'a shoot you, you old dumb nut.

RAY
Wow, Tiny, you almost scared me. You sure can hollar.

TINY
Yeah, man, I really can when somethin's after me.

LOU
C'mon, girl. C'mon in while I fix my hair.
(LOU's *hair is long and bushy, just having been washed. It covers her head like a gigantic crown*)

TINY (*Steps across* RAY)
Okay, girl. Hey, Ray, don't cha look up my dress.

RAY (*Jest*)
Why not, Tiny?

TINY
You must think you're gettin' big, boy.

RAY (*Drawl*)
I is.

LOU
Not that big, boy.

CLIFF
Why do you keep pesterin' the boy, Lou? If he didn't try and look I'd be wonderin' what's wrong with him.

LOU
Is that what you do, look?

CLIFF
What do you think?

(*Silence.*

CLARK *begins snuffling*)

LOU
The only thing that's wrong with Ray is you, Cliff. I know some of those nasty things you been tellin' him.

(Silence. LOU and CLIFF stare at each other)

TINY
I saw Doris and Bunny, Lou.
(Pause)
They said they'd be over. Said they had some business
to take care of.

(Pause)

CLARK
Doris comin' over?

TINY *(To CLARK)*
Yeah . . . yeah, stupid ass. She said she'd be down. And
Ray, Bunny said you'd better keep yo' ass home too.
She wants to ask you some questions about that girl
you been seein' out on "The Avenue."

RAY
What did she say?

CLIFF *(Grinning)*
So it's finally got back home.

LOU *(Hostile)*
Yeah, it's gotten back. You don't like it?

TINY
She said you'd better keep yo' black ass home, Ray.
That's what she said.

CLIFF *(Weary)*
Awww . . . Lou . . . please.

LOU
Followin' after you the way he does it's a wonder he
ain't always in some trouble.

CLIFF *(Caressing her leg)*
But, baby . . .

(She pulls her leg back)

RAY *(Angry)*
What she mean I better keep mah black ass home? I'll

go where I want . . . with who I want. She better watch it . . . or I won't be lettin' her come down here.

CLARK
Hey, listen to Tiger.

LOU
I ain't gonna let you start anything with little Bunny, you hear, Ray? Don't be hittin' on that little girl.

RAY
Awwww . . . sheeet.

LOU
What'd you say?

CLIFF
What'd it sound like he said?

LOU
Now you keep out of this, Cliff.

CLARK
You women folks are sho somethin' else.

TINY
You shut your mouth and mind your business, Clark.

LOU
Now listen here, Ray. Don't you talk to me like that, frownin' up your face an' rollin' yo' eyes. You gittin' too mannish 'round here. You hear?

(RAY *doesn't answer, but gives a deep sigh*)

Don't you bother that girl.

CLIFF
Ray?

RAY
Yeah?

CLIFF
If Bunny fucks with you . . . you knock her on her ass, ya hear?

RAY
Yeah, that's what I'm aimin' ta do, Cliff. Right on her ass.

(LOU *and* TINY *go in*)

CLARK
Hey, how 'bout pourin' me some of that wine you hidin' down there?

RAY
We ain't hidin' no wine.

CLIFF
Pour your own troubles, garbage gut.

CLARK
Why, hell, you ain't got nothin' here 'cept enough for maybe Ray here.

CLIFF
Ray, here? What do you mean "Ray here?" Why this youngblood nephew of mine will drink you underneath the table and into the middle of nex' week, ole Silly Willy Clark.

CLARK
Sheeet.

CLIFF
Can't you, Ray?

RAY *(Proudly)*
Sure as hell can.

CLARK
Well, we'll see . . . come on, let's go on up to the store and get us a big man.

RAY
A big man?

CLARK
That's right . . . a whole gallon.

(CLIFF *stands and beckons* RAY)

CLIFF
Never stand in the way of a man who wants to part
with some coins . . . and buy ya a drink at the same
time, I say.

CLARK
Yeah, c'mon . . .
     (As an afterthought)
. . . I'm buyin'.

CLIFF *(Humming)*
Hummmm hummm hummm . . . don't mind if I do get
a little refreshing night air . . . c'mon, Ray, let's take
a stroll.

CLARK
Well, which liquor store we goin' to? The one up on
"The Avenue" or the one down by the bridge?

CLIFF
Let's go up on "The Avenue."
     (Pause)
That's okay with you, Ray?

RAY
Yeah, fine with me.

CLARK
Boy, we gonna get pissy pukey fallin' down drunk tonight.

CLIFF
If you see your girl up on "The Avenue" you'll point
her out to me, Ray, won'tcha?

RAY
Yeah, Cliff. Yeah.

> *(They exit. The street is clear. Music plays, then
> a commercial begins.*
>
> *And lights down)*

CURTAIN

ACT III

Time: Forty-five minutes later.

Scene: Derby Street. LOU, TINY, DORIS, BUNNY GILLETTE, RED, and BAMA sit upon the Dawsons' stoop.

A gallon jug of red wine is on the pavement beside the steps, and everyone except RED and LOU has a paper cup in hand.

DORIS is a small girl, not as small as TINY, and has a full figure. RED looks like a hungry wolf and BAMA seems to be mostly elbows and knees.

LOU
I don't see how you folks drink that nasty ole muscatel wine.

DORIS *(Demonstrating)*
There's nothin' to it, baby sis.

RED
That's about the only goddamn thing we got in common, Lou. I don't drink that fucken hawg wash neither.

LOU *(Primly)*
If you must sit on my steps this late at night, Red, I wish you'd respect me and the other girls here by not bein' so foul mouthed.

RED *(Indignant)*
Shit, woman, talk to your ole man, Cliff . . . I'm usin' Mr. Dawson's rule book.

LOU
Don't blame Cliff!

BAMA *(To* RED)
Forget it, huh?

RED
You sometimes forget who your husband is, don't you, woman?

TINY
Yeah . . . knock it off, you guys.

RED *(To* TINY)
Fuck you, bitch!

LOU *(To* RED)
I got a good memory, little red nigger.

RED
So use it . . . and don't bug me.

BUNNY GILLETTE
If you fools gonna keep this up all night I'm goin'a go home!

BAMA
Bye!

LOU
But I got to live with Cliff, Red . . . not you . . . hear?

DORIS *(In high voice, nearly drunk)*
Do y'all want a hot dog? Do y'all want a hot dog?

TINY
Why don't we all stop arguing? I knew this would happen if you bought more wine, Bama.

BUNNY
You been drinkin' much as anybody.

BAMA
Ahhh, don't blame me. If I didn't get it somebody else would.

BUNNY
They up on "The Avenue" gettin' some more now.

LOU
Cliff and Ray's probably out lookin' for some ole funky bitches.

TINY
That's the way those punk-ass men are, girl.

BUNNY
Sho' is!

LOU
Who you callin' punk-ass?

TINY
Not anybody . . . well, I don't mean punk . . . it's just that all men are messed up.

BAMA
What chou talkin' 'bout, broad?

RED
Hey, Bama, you better straighten your ole lady out before I have to do it.

DORIS
Do y'all want a hot dog?

BUNNY
Yeah, who's this girl Ray's been seein', Lou?

LOU
Don't ask me, chile. Don't even let him know I said anything.

RED
Tell Ray I want to meet her, Bunny.

(BUNNY *threatens to pour her wine on him*)

TINY
When will Cliff be back?

DORIS
I said do y'all want a hot dog?

LOU
You waitin' for Cliff now, Tiny?

TINY
Yeah . . . Doris, I want one . . . but give them time to cook, will . . .

LOU
I asked you a question, Tiny.

TINY
Nawh . . . nawh . . . can't you see I'm with Bama. Ain't I, Bama?

RED *(Mutters)*
Goddamn . . . what a collection of cop-outs.

BAMA
Hey, get me a hot dog too.

DORIS
The mathafukkers should be done by now.

TINY *(Nervous laugh)*
Woman, stop usin' all that bad language. You know Lou don't like it.

DORIS
Shit on you and Lou both, it's my mouth.

LOU
Now I ain't gonna warn none of you no longer . . . Next one says one bad word has got to go home.

BAMA
Will you listen to this now?

RED
Hey, Doris, get me one of those fucken hot dogs, will ya?

LOU
That did it, Red . . . Go home!

RED
Okay.

TINY
Doris, you can't say two words without cussin'. Don't
you know any better?

RED *(Stands)*
But before I go, Lou, tell me what did I say that was
so bad?

LOU
I don't have to repeat it.

DORIS
I wouldn't be talkin' bout people so fucken much if I
was you, Tiny. Remember I know somethin' . . . now
don't I?

LOU
That goes for you too, Doris.

TINY *(Frightened)*
Whatta ya mean, Doris?

BUNNY
Uuuhhh uhhh . . . y'all sure do act funny when you
start in drinkin' this mess.

BAMA
Yeah . . . whatta ya mean, Doris?

DORIS
I ain't talkin' ta you, Bama.

BAMA
I'm talkin' ta you.
        (To TINY)
What she got on you, Mamma?

TINY
Whatta ya mean?

DORIS *(Drunk)*
Whatta ya think I mean?

BAMA
That's what I'm tryin' to find out . . . what ya mean.

RED
Shall we go . . . children?

TINY
That's what I'm askin' ya . . . whatta ya mean?

LOU
Now look. You broads can take that business back where you got it.

BAMA *(Amused)*
That's tellin' them, Lou.

TINY
Don't you be callin' me a broad!

BUNNY *(To* RED*)*
Red . . . don't you think . . .

RED
Shut up, woman!

LOU *(Amazed)*
Wha' . . . I didn't . . .

BAMA *(Joking)*
Yeah, you did. I hear you.

DORIS *(Jest)*
Don't be talkin' to mah baby sister like that.

TINY *(Scared and belligerent)*
What you gonna do 'bout it, bitch! You gonna tell her bout Cliff and me?

BAMA
Hey, cool it, baby.

LOU
What did you say?

BUNNY
Now Lou . . . don't get mad . . .

LOU *(Disgust)*
Okay, let's forget about it. You guys don't have to go home . . . I want you to wait on Cliff.

RED *(Sitting)*
Wasn't plannin' on goin', anyway.

LOU
Now looka hare, Red.

RED *(Angry)*
Goddammit! Make up your mind!

DORIS *(To* TINY*)*
You tryin' to be bad, ain't you, you li'l sawed-off heifer?

TINY *(Rising)*
Little heifer!

> (CLIFF, RAY *and* SILLY WILLY CLARK *turn the corner. They have a gallon jug of wine, half-emptied, which they pass between themselves and take large draughts.*
>
> *They visibly feel their drinks and stop under the streetlamp and drink and talk)*

CLIFF
Ray . . . just learn this one thing in life . . . When the time comes . . . be a man . . . however you've lived up till then . . . throw it out of your mind . . . Just do what you have to do as a man.

RAY *(Not sober)*
Sure, Cliff . . . sure.

CLARK *(Still drunker)*
That sho is right, Dawson . . . that's right . . . but why can't we be men all the time, Dawson?

CLIFF *(Annoyed)*
You don't know what I'm talkin' 'bout, silly ass, do you . . . do you now?

BUNNY
Here comes Cliff, Ray, and Silly Willy Clark.

DORIS *(Moving toward* TINY*)*
I'm tired of your little ass jumpin' bad around here, Tiny.

TINY *(Scared but standing her ground)*
You are?

BAMA *(Between them)*
Hey, knock off the bullshit . . . ya hear?

RED
Nawh, Bama . . . let them get it on and see who's the best.

TINY *(Crying)*
Bama, why you always takin' somebody's side against me?

LOU
Shut up, all of you!

BAMA
I'm not takin' nobody's side against you, baby.

DORIS
You ain't takin' my side, Bama? And what you callin' her baby fo'?

TINY *(To BAMA)*
Y'are!

BAMA
I ain't. We all just out to have a good time . . . that's all . . . a good time, huh?
> *(He pulls DORIS down beside him and puts his arm about her)*

TINY *(Scratching at his face)*
You bastard . . . I thought you was comin' down here to see me.

> (DORIS *pulls her small knife)*

LOU
Doris, stop!

DORIS
What the fuck's wrong with you, bitch!

(CLIFF comes up and sees DORIS's knife but doesn't appear to notice; she puts it away)

I'm goin' in an' get a hot dog.
(Same high voice)
Y'all want a hot dog?

(No answer. She enters the house.

BAMA, TINY, and LOU glare at each other. RED and BUNNY sit together)

RED
Well, if it ain't Mr. Dawson and nephew . . . the Derby Street killjoys. And hello, Mr. Silly Willy Clark . . . you simple mathafukker.

CLARK
Hey, everybody . . .
(Passing them the bottle)
. . . knock yourselves out.

BAMA
We got ours.

(LOU silently stands, looks at CLIFF and the drunken RAY and enters the house)

RED *(Hugs BUNNY, looks at RAY)*
Hey, what'cha mathafukkers doin'? Why don't you all have a sit down?

CLARK
Don't mind if I do, Red . . . Hey, Cliff, is it okay if I sit down on your steps?

CLIFF
Be my guest . . . you know me, don't you?

BUNNY *(Pulls away from RED)*
C'mon now, Red . . . stop all that stuff, man.

RED
You like it.
(He feels her breasts as they break)

LOU *(Looking out the door)*
I don't want to hear any more of that nasty shit from your mouth tonight, Red. And watch how you act!

RED
Watch how I act?

CLIFF
Yeah, that's what she said . . . watch how you act.

LOU
Yeah, you keep your hands to yourself. I saw that.

RED
Hey, what's wrong with you goddamn people tonight? Is there a full moon or somethin'?

BAMA
Hey, Red, let's split.

RED
Mr. and Mrs. Dawson . . . and nephew . . . I'm sorry. Forgive me. Will you please accept my humble-ass apology, huh? Will you Dawsons do that?
(RED *places his hand upon* LOU's *leg; she pulls away*)
Now what have I done?

BUNNY
What's wrong with you, Ray?

DORIS *(Sticks head out of door)*
Do y'all want a hot dog?

TINY
Ray's gone off somewhere behind that wine . . . look at him slobber spit . . . probably with his . . .

BUNNY
With his what?

TINY
Nothin', hon . . . I was just kiddin' . . .
(Shakes RAY)
. . . Wasn't I, Ray?

RAY
Yeah . . . yeah.

BAMA *(Mimics* DORIS)
"Do yawhl wants a hot dawg?"

TINY
Don't be so mean, Bama.

DORIS
Y'all can kiss mah ass.

LOU *(Caricature)*
Don't be so mean, Bama.

BAMA *(Furious)*
Who you tellin' to kiss your ass, woman? I thought
you saw what Bunny got tonight up on "The Avenue"
for . . .

      (MISS MINNY's *window goes up)*

TINY
Don't be so noisy, baby.

RED
I thought you was gonna get me one ah those mathafukkin' hot dogs, woman.

MISS MINNY
Cliff . . . Cliff . . . I see you out there . . . I'm callin'
the police right now about all this disturbance!
     (Her window goes down)

DORIS
You better watch your little self, Tiny.

LOU
I told you about your mouth, Red.

TINY
Watch myself?

RED
My mouth . . . awww . . . Lou. You can't be serious.

CLIFF
Well, children, it's time that Daddy got to bed . . . I suggest that everyone goes home to bed or just home. Good night, all.

LOU
Ain't you gonna stay out here and wait for the cops, Cliff?

CLIFF
Good night, my love. Don't be too long . . . I think your hair's sexy.

(LOU *has her hair in curlers.*

He goes in, followed by DORIS)

DORIS *(Off)*
Do y'all wants a hot dog, Cliff?

RED
If I hadn't seen Cliff beat so many bad niggers' asses I would think he's a chicken-hearted punk.

LOU
There's more than one way to be a coward.

BAMA
You better not let him hear you say that, lady.

CLARK
It's been a hard night, heh, Bunny?

BUNNY
Honey, these wine times is somethin' else.

RAY *(Mumbling)*
Sho is, baby. Sho is.

DORIS *(Back again, peering bleary-eyed at each one)*
Do y'all want a hot dog? Do y'all want a hot dog? If y'all don't, speak up . . . dese hare hot dogs gonna be all gone cause I'm eatin' them fast as I can.

RED
Shove 'em up your ass . . . you silly bitch.

LOU
Okay, you all have to go now!

> (RED *rises and is followed by the rest, except* RAY, *who snores on the step.* LOU *goes back into the house and her fussing with* CLIFF *about* RAY's *condition, his friends, and* TINY *can be more sensed than heard)*

BUNNY
Ray . . . Ray?

RAY
Yeah?

BUNNY
I gotta tell you somethin' . . . Ray? . . . Ray? . . . I got somethin' to tell ya.

BAMA
Leave him alone, Bunny.

TINY
Yeah, let him sleep. He'll find out.

RAY
Yeah . . . what is it?

BUNNY
I'm Red's girl now.

> (SILLY WILLY CLARK *gets up and enters the house)*

Did you hear me, Ray? Did you hear me?

> (RED *faces the building, and urinates in one of the wine bottles)*

RAY *(Groggy)*
Yeah . . . I heard you, Bunny. You're Red's girl now.

BAMA *(Giggling)*
I guess Ray's really got himself a new girl, Bunny.

> (RED *hands* RAY *the wine bottle he has just finished with)*

RED
Let's toast to that, Ray.

(Blindly, RAY *lifts the jug to his lips, as* BAMA *and* TINY *gasp)*

BUNNY
No! . . . No, Raayyy ! ! !
(She knocks the jug out of his grasp, smashing it upon the pavement. RAY *wakes instantly, perceives her action, and lashes out at her face. He lands a solid punch that knocks her sprawling in the street.*

RED *rushes* RAY *and hits him with a haymaker aside the head.* RAY *grabs him for support and the two fall to the pavement, grappling.*

TINY *screams. And* MISS MINNY's *window goes up.*

There are shouts and noise of running feet. The fighters roll about the pavement and BAMA *reaches down and pulls* RAY *off* RED *and holds him as the older boy smashes him in the face.*

SILLY WILLY CLARK *rushes from the house and grabs* BAMA *from behind. Upon his release from* BAMA, RAY *butts* RED *in the midriff and staggers him to the entrance of the alley.* RED *pulls a bone-handled switch-blade;* RAY *grabs his arm and they fight their way into the alley.*

DORIS *comes out of the house holding her small knife)*

DORIS *(To* BUNNY)
Where's Ray . . . Where's Ray!

*(*BUNNY, *dazed, points to the alley.* DORIS *enters the alley as* CLIFF *runs out of the door in only pants in time to see her disappear in the tunnel.*

The street is lit; the Krumps' upper windows are open)

EDDIE
Kill 'em . . . Kill 'em!

MRS. KRUMP
Keep back, Edward . . . there may be stray bullets!

> (SILLY WILLY CLARK *has choked* BAMA *into surrender)*

RED *(From the alley, muffled)*
All right . . . all right . . .

> *(As* CLIFF *runs into the alley there is a sharp sigh, then noise of more struggle and a groan.*
>
> LOU, TINY, BUNNY, *and Derby Street residents crowd around the alley entrance)*

MISS MINNY
Oh Lord . . . what's happened . . . what's happened?

MRS. KRUMP
Close the window, Edward . . . Close the window!

> *(The Krumps' window closes.*
>
> *The* POLICEMAN *turns the corner at a run)*

RESIDENT *(To another resident)*
Did you see what happen, Mr. Roy?

MR. ROY
Nawh, Miz Cooper . . . but I knew somethin' had to happen with all this goin' on down here.

> (RAY *emerges from the alley, blood on his shirt.* DORIS *follows him, her dress splotched with blood)*

THE POLICEMAN *(Running up with hand on pistol)*
What's happened here?

> (CLIFF *steps out of the alley, holding* RED's *knife)*

CLIFF *(Hands knife to* POLICEMAN *and points in alley)*
I killed him.

LOU *(Incredulous)*
You killed him . . .

(CLIFF *nods)*

RESIDENT
Did you hear that?

MISS MINNY
What happened? What happened, Miss Francis?

RESIDENT
Cliff Dawson's done killed a boy.

MISS MINNY
Ohhh . . . my Lord.

TINY *(Disbelief)*
You killed him?

THE POLICEMAN *(Leads* CLIFF *to stoop)*
Okay, everybody . . . get back and don't nobody leave.
By the looks of most of you . . . we'll want to talk to
you. Get back . . . Will somebody call an ambulance
and wagon?

MISS MINNY
I already did.

> (BAMA *has revived; he looks sick and sits
> beside the alley entrance.* BUNNY, CLARK *and*
> DORIS *support* RAY, *who looks to be in shock)*

LOU
Cliff . . . Cliff . . . don't do it . . . don't leave me! Tell
the truth.

(CLIFF *caresses her)*

CLIFF
It won't be for long . . . I was protectin' my family
. . . our family.

(LOU *cries, joining* TINY, BUNNY and one of *the neighbors.*

DORIS *appears resigned to the situation)*

RAY
She's gone ... she's gone ...

(A siren is heard)

DORIS
Who's gone, Ray? Who?

RAY
She is ... my girl ... my girl on "The Avenue."

DORIS
She'll be back.

RAY
No, she's not. She won't be back.

THE POLICEMAN
I have to warn you, Mr. Dawson, that anything you say can be used against you.

CLIFF *(Genuine)*
Yes, sir.

(BEATRICE *turns the corner)*

RAY
Never ... she'll never be back.

CLIFF
Lou ... Lou, I want one thing from you ...

(LOU *looks at him, then at* RAY)

LOU
He's all I got left, Cliff ... He's all the family I got left.

(He looks at her until she places her head upon his chest and sobs uncontrollably)

BEATRICE *(Walking up, to* MISS MINNY *in her window)*
What's the trouble, Miss Minny?

MISS MINNY
Ohhh, somethin' terrible, girl . . . I can't tell you now.

CLIFF *(Handcuffed to the* POLICEMAN)
It's your world, Ray . . . It's yours, boy . . . Go on out there and claim it.

(Sirens nearer. Lights down and music rises)

MISS MINNY
Come down tomorrow for tea, Beatrice, dear, and I'll tell you all about it.

BEATRICE
All right, Miss Minny. The Lord bless you tonight.

MISS MINNY
He will, dear . . . 'cause he works in mysterious ways.

BEATRICE *(Starting off)*
Amen!

(Lights down to blackness and a commercial begins)

CURTAIN

Gary Bolling as BOY, *Estelle Evans as* MOTHER, *Wayne Grice as* SON, *and Kelly-Marie Berry as* GIRL *in a scene from* A Son Come Home. *(Photo by Martha Holmes, courtesy of The American Place Theatre.)*

A SON,
COME HOME

A Son, Come Home was first produced at the American Place Theatre on March 26th, 1968. It was directed by Robert MacBeth, with scenery by John Jay Moore and lighting by Roger Morgan. The cast was as follows:

MOTHER, early 50's   Estelle Evans
SON, 30 years old   Wayne Grice
THE GIRL   Kelly-Marie Berry
THE BOY   Gary Bolling

Music for the production was composed by Gordon Watkins.

The BOY and the GIRL wear black tights and shirts. They move the action of the play and express the MOTHER's and the SON's moods and tensions. They become various embodiments recalled from memory and history: they enact a number of personalities and move from mood to mood.

The players are Black.

At rise: Scene: Bare stage but for two chairs positioned so as not to interfere with the actions of the BOY and the GIRL.

The MOTHER enters, sits in chair and begins to use imaginary iron and board. She hums a spiritual as she works.

MOTHER
You came three times . . . Michael? It took you three times to find me at home?

> (The GIRL enters, turns and peers through the cracked, imaginary door)

SON'S VOICE (Offstage)
Is Mrs. Brown home?

GIRL (An old woman)
What?

MOTHER
It shouldn't have taken you three times. I told you that I would be here by two and you should wait, Michael.

> (The SON enters, passes the GIRL and takes his seat upon the other chair.
>
> The BOY enters, stops on other side of the imaginary door and looks through at the GIRL)

BOY
Is Mrs. Brown in?

GIRL
Miss Brown ain't come in yet. Come back later . . .
She'll be in before dark.

MOTHER
It shouldn't have taken you three times . . . You should
listen to me, Michael. Standin' all that time in the cold.

SON
It wasn't cold, Mother.

MOTHER
I told you that I would be here by two and you should
wait, Michael.

BOY
Please tell Mrs. Brown that her son's in town to visit
her.

GIRL
You little Miss Brown's son? Well, bless the Lord.
(Calls over her shoulder)
Hey, Mandy, do you hear that? Little Miss Brown up-
stairs got a son . . . a great big boy . . . He's come to
visit her.

BOY
You'll tell her, won't you?

GIRL
Sure, I'll tell her.
(Grins and shows gums)
I'll tell her soon as she gets in.

MOTHER
Did you get cold, Michael?

SON
No, Mother. I walked around some . . . sightseeing.

BOY
I walked up Twenty-third Street toward South. I had
phoned that I was coming.

MOTHER
Sightseeing? But this is your home, Michael . . . always has been.

BOY
Just before I left New York I phoned that I was taking the bus. Two hours by bus, that's all. That's all it takes. Two hours.

SON
This town seems so strange. Different than how I remember it.

MOTHER
Yes, you have been away for a good while . . . How long has it been, Michael?

BOY
Two hours down the Jersey Turnpike, the trip beginning at the New York Port Authority Terminal . . .

SON
. . . and then straight down through New Jersey to Philadelphia . . .

GIRL
. . . and home . . . Just imagine . . . little Miss Brown's got a son who's come home.

SON
Yes, home . . . an anachronism.

MOTHER
What did you say, Michael?

BOY
He said . . .

GIRL (Late teens)
What's an anachronism, Mike?

SON
Anachronism: 1: an error in chronology; *esp:* a chronological misplacing of persons, events, objects, or

customs in regard to each other 2: a person or a thing
that is chronologically out of place—anachronistic/
also anachronic/ *or* anachronous—anachronistically/
also anachronously.

MOTHER
I was so glad to hear you were going to school in California.

BOY
College.

GIRL
Yes, I understand.

MOTHER
How long have you been gone, Michael?

SON
Nine years.

BOY
Nine years it's been. I wonder if she'll know me . . .

MOTHER
You've put on so much weight, son. You know that's
not healthy.

GIRL *(20 years old)*
And that silly beard . . . how . . .

SON
Oh . . . I'll take it off. I'm going on a diet tomorrow.

BOY
I wonder if I'll know her.

SON
You've put on some yourself, Mother.

MOTHER
Yes, the years pass. Thank the Lord.

BOY
I wonder if we've changed much.

GIRL
Yes, thank the Lord.

SON
The streets here seem so small.

MOTHER
Yes, it seems like that when you spend a little time in Los Angeles.

GIRL
I spent eighteen months there with your aunt when she was sick. She had nobody else to help her . . . she was so lonely. And you were in the service . . . away. You've always been away.

BOY
In Los Angeles the boulevards, the avenues, the streets . . .

SON
. . . are wide. Yes, they have some wide ones out West. Here, they're so small and narrow. I wonder how cars get through on both sides.

MOTHER
Why, you know how . . . we lived on Derby Street for over ten years, didn't we?

SON
Yeah, that was almost an alley.

MOTHER
Did you see much of your aunt before you left Los Angeles?

SON
What?

GIRL *(Middle-aged woman)* *(To* BOY)
Have you found a job yet, Michael?

MOTHER
Your aunt. My sister.

BOY
Nawh, not yet . . . Today I just walked downtown . . . quite a ways . . . this place is plenty big, ain't it?

SON
I don't see too much of Aunt Sophie.

MOTHER
But you're so much alike.

GIRL
Well, your bags are packed and are sitting outside the door.

BOY
My bags?

MOTHER
You shouldn't be that way, Michael. You shouldn't get too far away from your family.

SON
Yes, Mother.

BOY
But I don't have any money. I had to walk downtown today. That's how much money I have. I've only been here a week.

GIRL
I packed your bags, Michael.

MOTHER
You never can tell when you'll need or want your family, Michael.

SON
That's right, Mother.

MOTHER
You and she are so much alike.

BOY
Well, goodbye, Aunt Sophie.

A SON, COME HOME

GIRL
(Silence)

MOTHER
All that time in California and you hardly saw your aunt. My baby sister.

BOY
Tsk tsk tsk.

SON
I'm sorry, Mother.

MOTHER
In the letters I'd get from both of you there'd be no mention of the other. All these years. Did you see her again?

SON
Yes.

GIRL *(On telephone)*
Michael? Michael who? . . . Ohhh . . . Bernice's boy.

MOTHER
You didn't tell me about this, did you?

SON
No, I didn't.

BOY
Hello, Aunt Sophie. How are you?

GIRL
I'm fine, Michael. How are you? You're looking well.

BOY
I'm getting on okay.

MOTHER
I prayed for you.

SON
Thank you.

MOTHER
Thank the Lord, Michael.

BOY
Got me a job working for the city.

GIRL
You did now.

BOY
Yes, I've brought you something.

GIRL
What's this, Michael . . . ohhh . . . it's money.

BOY
It's for the week I stayed with you.

GIRL
Fifty dollars. But, Michael, you didn't have to.

MOTHER
Are you still writing that radical stuff, Michael?

SON
Radical?

MOTHER
Yes . . . that stuff you write and send me all the time in those little books.

SON
My poetry, Mother?

MOTHER
Yes, that's what I'm talking about.

SON
No.

MOTHER
Praise the Lord, son. Praise the Lord. Didn't seem like anything I had read in school.

BOY *(On telephone)*
Aunt Sophie? . . . Aunt Sophie? . . . It's me, Michael . . .

GIRL
Michael?

BOY
Yes . . . Michael . . .

GIRL
Oh . . . Michael . . . yes . . .

BOY
I'm in jail, Aunt Sophie . . . I got picked up for drunk driving.

GIRL
You did . . . how awful . . .

MOTHER
When you going to get your hair cut, Michael?

BOY
Aunt Sophie . . . will you please come down and sign my bail. I've got the money . . . I just got paid yester-day . . . They're holding more than enough for me . . . but the law says that someone has to sign for it.

MOTHER
You look almost like a hoodlum, Michael.

BOY
All you need to do is come down and sign . . . and I can get out.

MOTHER
What you tryin' to be . . . a savage or something? Are you keeping out of trouble, Michael?

GIRL
Ohhh . . . Michael . . . I'm sorry but I can't do nothin' like that . . .

BOY
But all you have to do is sign . . . I've got the money and everything.

GIRL
I'm sorry . . . I can't stick my neck out.

BOY

But, Aunt Sophie . . . if I don't get back to work I'll lose my job and everything . . . please . . .

GIRL

I'm sorry, Michael . . . I can't stick my neck out . . . I have to go now . . . Is there anyone I can call?

BOY

No.

GIRL

I could call your mother. She wouldn't mind if I reversed the charges on her, would she? I don't like to run my bills up.

BOY

No, thanks.

MOTHER

You and your aunt are so much alike.

SON

Yes, Mother. Our birthdays are in the same month.

MOTHER

Yes, that year was so hot . . . so hot and I was carrying you . . .

>   *(As the* MOTHER *speaks the* BOY *comes over and takes her by the hand and leads her from the chair, and they stroll around the stage, arm in arm.*
>
>   *The* GIRL *accompanies them and she and the* BOY *enact scenes from the* MOTHER's *mind)*

. . . carrying you, Michael . . . and you were such a big baby . . . kicked all the time. But I was happy. Happy that I was having a baby of my own . . . I worked as long as I could and bought you everything you might need . . . diapers . . . and bottles . . . and your own spoon . . . and even toys . . . and even books . . . And it was so hot in Philadelphia that year . . . Your Aunt Sophie used to come over and we'd go for walks . . . sometimes up on the avenue . . . I was living in West Philly then . . . in that old terrible section they called "The Bottom." That's where I met your father.

GIRL
You're such a fool, Bernice. No nigger . . . man or boy's . . . ever going to do a thing to me like that.

MOTHER
Everything's going to be all right, Sophia.

GIRL
But what is he going to do? How are you going to take care of a baby by yourself?

MOTHER
Everything's going to be all right, Sophia. I'll manage.

GIRL
You'll manage? How? Have you talked about marriage?

MOTHER
Oh, please, Sophia!

GIRL
What do you mean "please"? Have you?

MOTHER
I just can't. He might think . . .

GIRL
Think! That dirty nigger better think. He better think before he really messes up. And you better too. You got this baby comin' on. What are you going to do?

MOTHER
I don't know . . . I don't know what I can do.

GIRL
Is he still tellin' you those lies about . . .

MOTHER
They're not lies.

GIRL
Haaaa . . .

MOTHER
They're not.

GIRL
Some smooth-talkin' nigger comes up from Georgia and tell you he escaped from the chain gang and had to change his name so he can't get married 'cause they might find out . . . What kinda shit is that, Bernice?

MOTHER
Please, Sophia. Try and understand. He loves me. I I can't hurt him.

GIRL
Loves you . . . and puts you through this?

MOTHER
Please . . . I'll talk to him . . . Give me a chance.

GIRL
It's just a good thing you got a family, Bernice. It's just a good thing. You know that, don't cha?

MOTHER
Yes . . . yes, I do . . . but please don't say anything to him.

SON
I've only seen my father about a half dozen times that I remember, Mother. What was he like?

MOTHER
Down in The Bottom . . . that's where I met your father. I was young and hinkty then. Had big pretty brown legs and a small waist. Everybody used to call me Bernie . . . and me and my sister would go to At-lantic City on the weekends and work as waitresses in the evenings and sit all afternoon on the black part of the beach at Boardwalk and Atlantic . . . getting blacker . . . and having the times of our lives. Your

father probably still lives down in The Bottom . . .
perched over some bar down there . . . drunk to the
world . . . I can see him now . . . He had good white
teeth then . . . not how they turned later when he
started in drinkin' that wine and wouldn't stop . . .
he was so nice then.

BOY
Awwww, listen, kid. I got my problems too.

GIRL
But Andy . . . I'm six months gone . . . and you ain't
done nothin'.

BOY
Well, what can I do?

GIRL
Don't talk like that . . . What can you do? . . . You
know what you can do.

BOY
You mean marry you? Now lissen, sweetheart . . .

GIRL
But what about our baby?

BOY
Your baby.

GIRL
Don't talk like that! It took more than me to get him.

BOY
Well . . . look . . . I'll talk to you later, kid. I got to go
to work now.

GIRL
That's what I got to talk to you about too, Andy. I
need some money.

BOY
Money! Is somethin' wrong with your head, woman? I
ain't got no money.

GIRL
But I can't work much longer, Andy. You got to give me some money. Andy . . . you just gotta.

BOY
Woman . . . all I got to *ever* do is die and go to hell.

GIRL
Well, you gonna do that, Andy. You sho are . . . you know that, don't you? . . . You know that.

MOTHER
. . . Yes, you are, man. Praise the Lord. We all are . . . All of us . . . even though he ain't come for you yet to make you pay. Maybe he's waitin' for us to go together so I can be a witness to the retribution that's handed down. A witness to all that He'll bestow upon your sinner's head . . . A witness! . . . That's what I am, Andy! Do you hear me? . . . A witness!

SON
Mother . . . what's wrong? What's the matter?

MOTHER
Thank the Lord that I am not blinded and will see the fulfillment of divine . . .

SON
Mother!

MOTHER
Oh . . . is something wrong, Michael?

SON
You're shouting and walking around . . .

MOTHER
Oh . . . it's nothing, son. I'm just feeling the power of the Lord.

SON
Oh . . . is there anything I can get you, Mother?

MOTHER
No, nothing at all.
    (She sits again and irons)

SON
Where's your kitchen? . . . I'll get you some coffee . . . the way you like it. I bet I still remember how to fix it.

MOTHER
Michael . . . I don't drink anything like that no more.

SON
No?

MOTHER
Not since I joined the service of the Lord.

SON
Yeah? . . . Well, do you mind if I get myself a cup?

MOTHER
Why, I don't have a kitchen. All my meals are prepared for me.

SON
Oh . . . I thought I was having dinner with you.

MOTHER
No. There's nothing like that here.

SON
Well, could I take you out to a restaurant? . . . Remember how we used to go out all the time and eat? I've never lost my habit of liking to eat out. Remember . . . we used to come down to this part of town and go to restaurants. They used to call it home cooking then . . . now, at least where I been out West and up in Harlem . . . we call it soul food. I bet we could find a nice little restaurant not four blocks from here, Mother. Remember that old man's place we used to go to on Nineteenth and South? I bet he's dead now . . . but . . .

MOTHER
I don't even eat out no more, Michael.

SON
No?

MOTHER
Sometimes I take a piece of holy bread to work . . . or
some fruit . . . if it's been blessed by my Spiritual
Mother.

SON
I see.

MOTHER
Besides . . . we have a prayer meeting tonight.

SON
On Friday?

MOTHER
Every night. You'll have to be going soon.

SON
Oh.

MOTHER
You're looking well.

SON
Thank you.

MOTHER
But you look tired.

SON
Do I?

MOTHER
Yes, those rings around your eyes might never leave.
Your father had them.

SON
Did he?

MOTHER
Yes . . . and cowlicks . . . deep cowlicks on each side
of his head.

SON
Yes . . . I remember.

MOTHER
Do you?

> *(The* BOY *and the* GIRL *take crouching posi-*
> *tions behind and in front of them. They are in a*
> *streetcar. The* BOY *behind the* MOTHER *and*
> SON, *the* GIRL *across the aisle, a passenger)*

MOTHER *(Young woman) (To the* BOY)
Keep your damn hands off him, Andy!

BOY *(Chuckles)*
Awww, c'mon . . . Bernie. I ain't seen him since he was
in the crib.

MOTHER
And you wouldn't have seen neither of us . . . if I had
anything to do with it . . . Ohhh . . . why did I get on
this trolley?

BOY
C'mon . . . Bernie . . . don't be so stuckup.

MOTHER
Don't even talk to us . . . and stop reaching after him.

BOY
Awww . . . c'mon . . . Bernie. Let me look at him.

MOTHER
Leave us alone. Look . . . people are looking at us.

> *(The* GIRL *across the aisle has been peeking at*
> *the trio but looks toward front at the mention of*
> *herself)*

BOY
Hey, big boy . . . do you know who I am?

MOTHER
Stop it, Andy! Stop it, I say . . . Mikie . . . don't pay
any attention to him . . . you hear?

BOY
Hey, big boy . . . know who I am? . . . I'm your
daddy. Hey, there . . .

MOTHER
Shut up . . . shut up, Andy . . . you nothin' to us.

BOY
Where you livin' at . . . Bernie? Let me come on by and see the little guy, huh?

MOTHER
No! You're not comin' near us . . . ever . . . you hear?

BOY
But I'm his father . . . look . . . Bernie . . . I've been an ass the way I've acted but . . .

MOTHER
He ain't got no father.

BOY
Oh, come off that nonsense, woman.

MOTHER
Mikie ain't got no father . . . his father's dead . . . you hear?

BOY
Dead?

MOTHER
Yes, dead. My son's father's dead.

BOY
What you talkin' about? . . . He's the spittin' image of me.

MOTHER
Go away . . . leave us alone, Andrew.

BOY
See there . . . he's got the same name as me. His first name is Michael after your father . . . and Andrew after me.

MOTHER
No, stop that, you hear?

BOY
Michael Andrew . . .

MOTHER
You never gave him no name . . . his name is Brown
. . . Brown. The same as mine . . . and my sister's . . .
and my daddy . . . You never gave him nothin' . . . and
you're dead . . . go away and get buried.

BOY
You know that trouble I'm in . . . I got a wife down
there, Bernie. I don't care about her . . . what could I
do?

MOTHER *(Rises, pulling up the* SON)
We're leavin' . . . don't you try and follow us . . . you
hear, Andy? C'mon . . . Mikie . . . watch your step now.

BOY
Well . . . bring him around my job . . . you know where
I work. That's all . . . bring him around on payday.

MOTHER *(Leaving)*
We don't need anything from you . . . I'm working . . .
just leave us alone.

(The BOY *turns to the* GIRL)

BOY *(Shrugs)*
That's the way it goes . . . I guess. Ships passing on
the trolley car . . . Hey . . . don't I know you from up
around 40th and Market?

(The GIRL *turns away)*

SON
Yeah . . . I remember him. He always had liquor on his
breath.

MOTHER
Yes . . . he did. I'm glad that stuff ain't got me no
more . . . Thank the Lord.

GIRL *(35 years old)*
You want to pour me another drink, Michael?

A SON, COME HOME   205

BOY *(15 years old)*
You drink too much, Mother.

GIRL
Not as much as some other people I know.

BOY
Well, me and the guys just get short snorts, Mother.
But you really hide some port.

GIRL
Don't forget you talkin' to your mother. You gettin'
more like your father every day.

BOY
Is that why you like me so much?

GIRL *(Grins drunkenly)*
Oh, hush up now, boy . . . and pour me a drink.

BOY
There's enough here for me too.

GIRL
That's okay . . . when Will comes in he'll bring something.

SON
How is Will, Mother?

MOTHER
I don't know . . . haven't seen Will in years.

SON
Mother.

MOTHER
Yes, Michael.

SON
Why you and Will never got married? . . . You stayed
together for over ten years.

MOTHER
Oh, don't ask me questions like that, Michael.

SON
But why not?

MOTHER
It's just none of your business.

SON
But you could be married now . . . not alone in this
room . . .

MOTHER
Will had a wife and child in Chester . . . you know that.

SON
He could have gotten a divorce, Mother . . . Why . . .

MOTHER
Because he just didn't . . . that's why.

SON
You never hear from him?

MOTHER
Last I heard . . . Will had cancer.

SON
Oh, he did.

MOTHER
Yes.

SON
Why didn't you tell me? . . . You could have written.

MOTHER
Why?

SON
So I could have known.

MOTHER
So you could have known? Why?

SON
Because Will was like a father to me . . . the only one
I've really known.

A SON, COME HOME   207

MOTHER
A father? And you chased him away as soon as you got big enough.

SON
Don't say that, Mother.

MOTHER
You made me choose between you and Will.

SON
Mother.

MOTHER
The quarrels you had with him . . . the mean tricks you used to play . . . the lies you told to your friends about Will . . . He wasn't much . . . when I thought I had a sense of humor I us'ta call him just plain Will. But we was his family.

SON
Mother, listen.

MOTHER
And you drove him away . . . and he didn't lift a hand to stop you.

SON
Listen, Mother.

MOTHER
As soon as you were big enough you did all that you could to get me and Will separated.

SON
Listen.

MOTHER
All right, Michael . . . I'm listening.

(Pause)

SON
Nothing.

(Pause. Lifts an imaginary object)
Is this your tambourine?

MOTHER
Yes.

SON
Do you play it?

MOTHER
Yes.

SON
Well?

MOTHER
Everything I do in the service of the Lord I do as well
as He allows.

SON
You play it at your meetings.

MOTHER
Yes, I do. We celebrate the life He has bestowed upon
us.

SON
I guess that's where I get it from.

MOTHER
Did you say something, Michael?

SON
Yes. My musical ability.

MOTHER
Oh . . . you've begun taking your piano lessons again?

SON
No . . . I was never any good at that.

MOTHER
Yes, three different teachers and you never got past
the tenth lesson.

A SON, COME HOME

SON
You have a good memory, Mother.

MOTHER
Sometimes, son. Sometimes.

SON
I play an electric guitar in a combo.

MOTHER
You do? That's nice.

SON
That's why I'm in New York. We got a good break and came East.

MOTHER
That's nice, Michael.

SON
I was thinking that Sunday I could rent a car and come down to get you and drive you up to see our show. You'll get back in plenty of time to rest for work Monday.

MOTHER
No, I'm sorry. I can't do that.

SON
But you would like it, Mother. We could have dinner up in Harlem, then go down and . . .

MOTHER
I don't do anything like that any more, Michael.

SON
You mean you wouldn't come to see me play even if I were appearing here in Philly?

MOTHER
That's right, Michael. I wouldn't come. I'm past all that.

SON
Oh, I see.

MOTHER
Yes, thank the Lord.

SON
But it's my life, Mother.

MOTHER
Good . . . then you have something to live for.

SON
Yes.

MOTHER
Well, you're a man now, Michael . . . I can no longer
live it for you. Do the best with what you have.

SON
Yes . . . Yes, I will, Mother.

GIRL'S VOICE *(Offstage)*
Sister Brown . . . Sister Brown . . . hello.

MOTHER *(Uneasy; peers at watch)*
Oh . . . it's Mother Ellen . . . I didn't know it was so
late.

GIRL *(Enters)*
Sister Brown . . . how are you this evening?

MOTHER
Oh, just fine, Mother.

GIRL
Good. It's nearly time for dinner.

MOTHER
Oh, yes, I know.

GIRL
We don't want to keep the others waiting at meeting
. . . do we?

MOTHER
No, we don't.

GIRL *(Self-assured)*
Hello, son.

A SON, COME HOME   211

SON
Hello.

MOTHER
Oh, Mother . . . Mother . . .

GIRL
Yes, Sister Brown, what is it?

MOTHER
Mother . . . Mother . . . this is . . . this is . . .
(Pause)
. . . this is . . .

SON
Hello, I'm Michael. How are you?

MOTHER *(Relieved)*
Yes, Mother . . This is Michael . . . my son.

GIRL
Why, hello, Michael. I've heard so much about you from your mother. She prays for you daily.

SON *(Embarrassed)*
Oh . . . good.

GIRL *(Briskly)*
Well . . . I have to be off to see about the others.

MOTHER
Yes, Mother Ellen.

GIRL *(As she exits; chuckles)*
Have to tell everyone that you won't be keeping us waiting, Bernice.

(Silence)

SON
Well, I guess I better be going, Mother.

MOTHER
Yes.

SON
I'll write.

MOTHER
Please do.

SON
I will.

MOTHER
You're looking well ... Thank the Lord.

SON
Thank you, so are you, Mother.
        (He moves toward her and hesitates)

MOTHER
You're so much like your aunt. Give her my best . . .
won't you?

SON
Yes, I will, Mother.

MOTHER
Take care of yourself, son.

SON
Yes, Mother. I will.
        (The SON *exits. The* MOTHER *stands looking
        after him as the lights go slowly down to . . .)*

BLACKNESS

A scene from The Electronic Nigger and Others. *(Photo by Martha Holmes, cou tesy of The American Place Theatre.)*

THE
ELECTRONIC
NIGGER

A Tragi-Comedy

The Electronic Nigger was first produced at the American Place Theatre on March 26, 1968. The production was directed by Robert MacBeth. Sets were designed by John Jay Moore, lighting by Roger Morgan. The cast was as follows:

MR. JONES	Wayne Grice
LENARD	Warren Pincus
MISS MOSKOWITZ	Jeanne Kaplan
MR. CARPENTIER	L. Errol Jaye
BILL	Roscoe Orman
SUE	Hedy Sontag
MARTHA	Helen Ellis
STUDENTS	Ronald A. Hirsch
	Maie Mottus

MR. JONES: A light-brown-skinned man. Thirty years old. Hornrimmed glasses. Crewcut and small, smart mustache. He speaks in a clipped manner when in control of himself but is more than self-conscious, even from the beginning. Whatever, MR. JONES speaks as unlike the popular conception of how a negro speaks as is possible. Not even the fallacious accent acquired by many "cultured" or highly educated negroes should be sought, but that general cross-fertilized dialect found on various Ivy League and the campuses of the University of California. He sports an ascot.

MR. CARPENTIER: A large, dark man in his late thirties. He speaks in blustering orations, many times mispronouncing words. His tone is stentorian, and his voice has an absurdly ridiculous affected accent.

BILL: Twenty-two years old. Negro.

SUE: Twenty years old. White.

LENARD: Twenty-one. A fat white boy.

MISS MOSKOWITZ: Mid-thirties. An aging professional student.

MARTHA: An attractive negro woman.

Any number of interracial students to supply background, short of the point of discouraging a producer.

Scene: A classroom of a Southern California junior college.

Modern decor. New facilities:

Light green blackboards, bright fluorescent lighting, elongated rectangular tables, seating four to eight students, facing each other, instead of the traditional rows of seats facing toward the instructor. The tables are staggered throughout the room and canted at angles impossible for the instructor to engage the eye of the student, unless the student turns toward him or the instructor leaves his small table and walks among the students.

It is seven o'clock by the wall-clock; twilight outside the windows indicates a fall evening. A NO SMOKING sign is beneath the clock, directly above the green blackboards, behind the instructor's table and rostrum.

The bell rings.

Half the STUDENTS are already present. MISS MOSKOWITZ drinks coffee from a paper cup; LENARD munches an apple, noisily. More STUDENTS enter from the rear and front doors to the room and take seats. There is the general low buzz of activity and first night anticipation of a new evening class.

BILL comes in the back door to the room; SUE enters the other. THEY casually look about them for seats and indifferently sit next to each other.

JONES enters puffing on his pipe and smoothing down his ascot.

The bell rings.

MR. JONES *(Exhaling smoke)*
Well . . . good evening . . . My name is Jones . . . ha ha . . . that won't be hard to remember, will it? I'll be your instructor this semester . . . ha ha . . . Now this is English 22E . . . Creative Writing.

LENARD
Did you say 22E?

MR. JONES
Yes, I did . . . Do all of you have that number on your cards? . . . Now look at your little I.B.M. cards and see if there is a little 22E in the upper left hand corner. Do you see it?

> (CARPENTIER *enters and looks over the class*)

MISS MOSKOWITZ *(Confused)*
Why . . . I don't see any numbers on my card.

MR. JONES *(Extinguishing pipe)*
Good . . . now that everyone seems to belong here who is here, we can get started with our creativity . . . ha ha . . . If I sort of . . .

MISS MOSKOWITZ *(Protesting)*
But I don't have a number!

LENARD *(Ridicule)*
Yes, you do!

MISS MOSKOWITZ
Give that back to me . . . give that card back to me right now!

LENARD *(Pointing to card)*
It's right here like he said . . . in the upper left-hand corner.

MISS MOSKOWITZ *(Snatching card)*
I know where it is!

MR. JONES
Now that we all know our . . .

MR. CARPENTIER
Sir . . . I just arrived in these surroundings and I have
not yet been oriented as to the primary sequence of
events which have preceded my entrance.

MR. JONES
Well, nothing has . . .

MR. CARPENTIER *(Cutting)*
If you will enlighten me I'll be eternally grateful for
any communicative aid that you may render in your
capacity as professor *de la classe*.

MR. JONES
Well . . . well . . . I'm not a professor, I'm an instructor.

BILL
Just take a look at your card and see if. . .

MR. CARPENTIER
Didn't your mother teach you any manners, young
man?

BILL
What did you say, fellah?

MR. CARPENTIER
Don't speak until you're asked to . . .

MR. JONES
Now you people back there . . . pay attention.

MISS MOSKOWITZ
Why, I never in all my life . . .

MR. JONES
Now to begin with . . .

SUE
You've got some nerve speaking to him like that.
Where did you come from, mister?

MR. JONES
Class!

MR. CARPENTIER
Where I came from . . . *mon bonne femme* . . . has no
bearing on this situational conundrum . . . splendid
word, conundrum, heh, what? Jimmie Baldwin uses it
brilliantly on occasion . . .

MR. JONES
I'm not going to repeat . . .

MR. CARPENTIER
But getting back to the matter at hand . . . I am here
to become acquainted with the formal aspects of au-
thorcraft . . . Of course I've been a successful writer
for many years even though I haven't taken the time
for the past ten years to practice the art-forms of fiction, drama or that very breath of the muse . . .
poesy . . .

MR. JONES
Sir . . . please!

BILL
How do you turn it off?

LENARD
For christ sake!

MR. CARPENTIER
But you can find my name footnoted in numerous professional   sociological-psychological-psychiatric   and
psychedelic journals . . .

MR. JONES
If you'll please . . .

MR. CARPENTIER
A. T. Carpentier is the name . . . notice the silent T . . .
My profession gets in the way of art, in the strict
aesthetic sense, you know . . . I'm a Sociological Data
Research Analysis Technician Expert. Yes, penal-
ology is my field, naturally, and I have been in over
thirty-three penal institutions across the country . . .
in a professional capacity, obviously . . . ha ho ho.

MR. JONES
Sir!

LENARD
Geez!

MR. CARPENTIER
Here are some of my random findings, conclusions, etc.
which I am re-creating into a new art-form . . .

SUE
A new art-form we have here already.

BILL
This is going to be one of those classes.

MR. CARPENTIER
Yes, young lady . . . Socio Drama . . .

MR. JONES
All right, Mr. Carpenter.

MR. CARPENTIER *(Corrects)*
Carpentier! The T is silent.

MR. JONES
Okay. Complete what you were saying. . . .

MR. CARPENTIER
Thank you, sir.

MR. JONES
. . . and then . . .

MR. CARPENTIER
By the way, my good friend J. J. Witherthorn is al-

ready dickering with my agent for options on my finished draft for a pilot he is planning to shoot of *Only Corpses Beat the Big House* which, by the way, is the title of the first script, taken from an abortive *novella narratio* I had begun in my youth after a particularly torrid affair with one Eulah Mae Jackson . . .

MR. JONES
Good . . . now let's . . .

MR. CARPENTIER
Of course, after I read it some of you will say it resembles in some ways *The Quare Fellow,* but I have documented evidence that I've had this plot outlined since . . .

BILL
Question!

SUE
Won't somebody do something?

BILL
Question!

MR. JONES *(To* BILL)
Yes, what is it?

MR. CARPENTIER *(Over)*
. . . Of course I'll finish it on time . . . the final draft, I mean . . . and have it to J. J. far ahead of the deadline but I thought that the rough edges could be chopped off here . . . and there . . .

MR. JONES *(Approaching anger)*
Mr. Carpentier . . . if you'll please?

MR. CARPENTIER *(Belligerent and glaring)*
I beg your pardon, sir?

(MARTHA *enters)*

MR. JONES
This class must get under way . . . immediately!

THE ELECTRONIC NIGGER   223

MARTHA *(To* MR. JONES)
Is this English 22E?

MR. CARPENTIER
Why, yes, you are in the correct locale, *mon jeune fil.*

MR. JONES
May I see your card, Miss?

MR. CARPENTIER *(Mutters)*
Intrusion ... non-equanimity ...

MISS MOSKOWITZ
Are you speaking to me?

MR. JONES *(To* MARTHA)
I believe you're in the right class, miss.

MARTHA
Thank you.

MR. JONES *(Clears throat)*
Hummp ... huump ... well, we can get started now.

MR. CARPENTIER
I emphatically agree with you, sir. In fact ...

MR. JONES *(Cutting)*
Like some of you, I imagine, this too is my first evening class ... And I'd ...

MISS MOSKOWITZ *(Beaming)*
How nice!

LENARD
Oh ... oh ... we've got a green one.

MR. JONES
Well . . . I guess the first thing is to take the roll. I
haven't the official roll sheet yet, so ...
. . . please print your names clearly on this sheet of
paper and pass it around so you'll get credit for being
here tonight.

BILL
Question!

MR. JONES
Yes . . . you did have a question, didn't you?

BILL
Yeah . . . How will we be graded?

SUE
Oh . . . how square!

MR. JONES *(Smiling)*
I'm glad you asked that.

MISS MOSKOWITZ
So am I.

LENARD
You are?

MR. JONES
Well . . . as of now everybody is worth an A. I see all students as A students until they prove otherwise . . .

MISS MOSKOWITZ
Oh, how nice.

MR. JONES
But tonight I'd like us to talk about story ideas. Since this is a writing class we don't wish to waste too much of our time on matters other than writing. And it is my conclusion that a story isn't a story without a major inherent idea which gives it substance . . .

MISS MOSKOWITZ
How true.

MR. JONES
And, by the way, that is how you are to retain your A's. By handing in all written assignments on time and doing the necessary outside work . . .

LENARD
Typewritten or in longhand, Mr. Jones?

MR. JONES
I am not a critic, so you will not be graded on how well

you write but merely if you attempt to grow from the experience you have in this class . . . this class is not only to show you the fundamentals of fiction, drama and poetry but aid your productivity, or should I say creativity . . . ha ha . . .

MR. CARPENTIER *(Admonishing)*
You might say from the standpoint of grammar that fundamentals are essential but . . .

MR. JONES *(Piqued)*
Mr. Carpentier . . . I don't understand what point you are making!

MR. CARPENTIER *(Belligerent)*
Why . . . why . . . you can say that without the basics of grammar, punctuation, spelling, etc. . . . that these neophytes will be up the notorious creek without even the accommodation of a sieve.

SUE
Jesus!

LENARD *(Scowling)*
Up the where, buddy?

MISS MOSKOWITZ
I don't think we should . . .

BILL
It's fantastic what you . . .

MARTHA
Is this really English 22E?

MR. JONES
Now wait a minute, class. Since this is the first night, I want everyone to identify themselves before they speak. All of you know my name . . .

MARTHA
I don't, sir.

MR. CARPENTIER
You might say they will come to grief . . . artistic calamity.

MR. JONES
Ohhh ... It's Jones ... Ray Jones.

LENARD
Didn't you just publish a novel, Mr. Jones?

MARTHA
Mine's Martha ... Martha Butler.

MR. JONES
Oh, yes ... yes, a first novel.

MR. CARPENTIER *(Mutters)*
Cultural lag's the real culprit!

BILL *(To* SUE)
I'm Bill ... Bill Cooper.

SUE
Pleased ... just call me Sue. Susan Gold.

MR. JONES
Now ... where were we? ...

MR. CARPENTIER
In the time of classicism there wasn't this rampant
commerce among Philistines ...

MR. JONES
Does someone ...

MISS MOSKOWITZ
Story ideas, Mr. Jones.

MR. JONES
Oh, yes.

> *(Hands are raised.* LENARD *is pointed out)*

LENARD
I have an idea for a play.

MR. JONES
Your name, please.

LENARD
Lenard ... Lenard Getz. I have an idea for a lavish
stage spectacle using just one character.

THE ELECTRONIC NIGGER   227

MR. CARPENTIER
It won't work ... it won't work!

SUE
How do you know?

MISS MOSKOWITZ
Let Lenard tell us, will ya?

MR. CARPENTIER *(Indignant)*
Let him! Let him, you say!

MR. JONES *(Annoyed)*
Please, Mr. Carpentier ... please be ...

MR. CARPENTIER *(Glaring about the room)*
But I didn't say it had to be done as parsimoniously as
a Russian play. I mean only as beginners you people
should delve into the simplicity of the varied tech-
niques of the visual communicative media and proc-
esses.

MR. JONES
For the last time ...

MR. CARPENTIER
Now take for instance cinema ... or a tele-drama ...
some of the integrative shots set the mood and that
takes technique as well as craft.

MR. JONES
I have my doubts about all that ... but it doesn't have
anything to do with Lenard's idea, as I see it.

MR. CARPENTIER
I don't agree with you, sir.

MR. JONES
It's just as well that you don't. Lenard, will you go on,
please?

LENARD
Ahhh ... forget it.

MR. JONES
But, Lenard, won't you tell us your idea?

LENARD
No!

MISS MOSKOWITZ
Oh . . . Lenard.

MR. CARPENTIER
There is a current theory about protein variation . . .

MR. JONES
Not again!

SUE *(Cutting)*
I have a story idea!

MISS MOSKOWITZ
Good!

MR. JONES
Can we hear it . . . Miss . . . Miss . . . ?

SUE
Miss Gold. Susan Gold.

MR. JONES
Thank you.

SUE
Well, it's about a story that I have in my head. It ends
with a girl or woman, standing or sitting alone and
frightened. It's weird. I don't know where I got *that*
theme from! . . . There is just something about one
person, alone, that is moving to me. It's the same thing
in movies or in photography. Don't you think if it's
two or more persons, it loses a dramatic impact?

MR. JONES
Why, yes, I do.

MISS MOSKOWITZ
It sounds so psychologically pregnant!

LENARD
It's my story of the stupendous one-character extrava-
ganza!

(A few in the class hesitantly clap)

MR. CARPENTIER *(In a deep, pontifical voice)*
Loneliness! Estrangement! Alienation! The young lady's story should prove an interesting phenomena— it is a phenomena that we observe daily.

MISS MOSKOWITZ
Yes, it is one of the most wonderful things I've ever heard.

MR. JONES *(Irritated)*
Well, now let's . . .

MR. CARPENTIER
The gist of that matter . . .

MR. JONES
I will not have any more interruptions, man. Are you all there!

MR. CARPENTIER
I mean only to say that it is strictly in a class of phenomenology in the classic ontonological sense.

MR. JONES
There are rules you must observe, Mr. Carpentier. Like our society, this school too has rules.

MR. CARPENTIER
Recidivism! Recidivism!

MARTHA
Re-sida-what?

MR. CARPENTIER *(Explaining)*
Recidivism. A noted example of alienation in our society. We have tape-recorded AA meetings without the patients knowing that they were being recorded. In prison we pick up everything . . . from a con pacing his cell . . . down to the fights in the yard . . . and I can say that the milieu which creates loneliness is germane to the topic of recidivism.

MR. JONES
What? . . . You're a wire-tapper, Mr. Carpentier?

MR. CARPENTIER
Any method that deters crime in our society is most
inadequate, old boy.

BILL
A goddamned fink!

LENARD
I thought I smelled somethin'.

MR. CARPENTIER
Crime is a most repetitive theme these days. . . . The
primacy purpose of we law enforcement agents is to
help stamp it out whatever the method.

MR. JONES
Carpentier!

MR. CARPENTIER
Let the courts worry about . . .

MR. JONES
But, sir, speaking man to man, how do you feel about
your job? Doesn't it make you uneasy knowing that
your race, I mean, our people, the Negro, is the most
victimized by the police in this country? And you are
using illegal and immoral methods to . . .

MR. CARPENTIER
Well, if you must personalize that's all right with me
. . . but, really, I thought this was a class in creative
writing, not criminology. I hesitate to say, Mr. Jones,
that you are indeed out of your depth when you engage
me on my own grounds . . . ha ha . . .

>   (MR. JONES *has taken off his glasses and is
>   looking at* MR. CARPENTIER *strangely.*)

MARTHA *(Raising voice)*
I have a story idea . . . it's about this great dark mass
of dough . . .

BILL
Yeah . . . like a great rotten ham that strange rumbling
and bubbling noises come out of . . .

SUE
And it stinks something awful!

LENARD
Like horseshit!

MISS MOSKOWITZ
Oh, my.

MR. JONES
Class! Class!

MR. CARPENTIER *(Oblivious)*
The new technology doesn't allow for the weak tyranny of human attitudes.

MR. JONES
You are wrong, terribly wrong.

MR. CARPENTIER
This is the age of the new intellectual assisted by his tool, the machine, I'll have you know!

MR. JONES *(Furious)*
Carpentier! . . . That is what we are here in this classroom to fight against . . . we are here to discover, to awaken, to search out human values through art!

MR. CARPENTIER
Nonsense! Nonsense! Pure nonsense! All you pseudo-artistic types and humanists say the same things when confronted by truth.
  (Prophetically)
This is an age of tele-symbology . . . phallic in nature, oral in appearance.

MR. JONES
Wha' . . . I don't believe I follow you. Are you serious, man?

MR. CARPENTIER
I have had more experience with these things so I can say that the only function of cigarettes is to show the cigarette as a symbol of gratification for oral types . . .

Tobacco, matches, Zig Zag papers, etc. are all barter items in prison. There you will encounter a higher incident of oral and anal specimens. I admit it is a liberal interpretation, true, but I don't see how any other conclusion can be drawn!

MR. JONES
You are utterly ineducable. I suggest you withdraw from this class, Mr. Carpentier.

MISS MOSKOWITZ
Oh, how terrible.

BILL
Hit the road, Jack.

MR. CARPENTIER
If I must call it to your attention . . . in a tax-supported institution . . . to whom does that institution belong?

LENARD
That won't save you, buddy.

MR. JONES
Enough of this! Are there any more story ideas, class?

MR. CARPENTIER *(Mumbling)*
It's councilmatic . . . yes, councilmatic . . .

MISS MOSKOWITZ
My name is Moskowitz and I'd like to try a children's story.

MR. CARPENTIER
Yes, yes, F. G. Peters once sold a story to the Howdie Dowdie people on an adaptation of the *Cherry Orchard* theme . . . and Jamie Judson, a good friend of mine . . .

MR. JONES
Mr. Carpentier . . . please. Allow someone else a chance.

MR. CARPENTIER
Why, all they have to do is speak up, Mr. Jones.

MR. JONES
Maybe so . . . but please let Mrs. Moskowitz . . .

MISS MOSKOWITZ *(Coyly)*
That's Miss Moskowitz, Mr. Jones.

MR. JONES
Oh, I'm sorry, Miss Moskowitz.

MISS MOSKOWITZ
That's okay, Mr. Jones ... Now my story has an historical background.

MR. CARPENTIER
Which reminds me of a story I wrote which had a setting in colonial Boston ...

LENARD
Not again. Not again, for chrissakes!

MR. CARPENTIER
Christopher Attucks was the major character ...

SUE
Shhhhhh ...

BILL
Shut up, fellow!

MR. CARPENTIER *(Ignoring them)*
The whole thing was done in jest ... the historical inaccuracies were most hilarious ... ha ho ho ...

MR. JONES
Mr. Carpentier ! ! !

(MR. CARPENTIER *grumbles and glowers)*

MISS MOSKOWITZ
Thank you, Mr. Jones.

MR. JONES
That's quite all right ... go on, please.

MISS MOSKOWITZ
Yes, now this brother and sister are out in a park and they get separated from their mother and meet a lion escaped from the zoo and make friends with him.

LENARD
And they live happily ever afterwards.

MISS MOSKOWITZ
Why, no, not at all, Lenard. The national guard comes to shoot the lion but the children hide him up a tree.

BILL *(To* SUE)
I got the impression that it was a tall tale.

SUE
Not you too?

LENARD
I thought it had a historical background.

MARTHA
Can you convince children that they can easily make friends out of lions and then hide them up trees?

LENARD
I got that it's pretty clear what motivated the lion to climb the tree. If you had a hunting party after you wouldn't . . .

MR. CARPENTIER *(Cutting)*
Unless you give the dear lady that liberty . . . you'll end up with merely thous and thees!

MR. JONES
What?

MISS MOSKOWITZ *(Simpering)*
Oh, thank you, Mr. Carpentier.

MR. CARPENTIER *(Beau Brummel)*
Why, the pleasure is all mine, dear lady.

MR. JONES
Enough of this! Enough of this!

MISS MOSKOWITZ *(Blushing)*
Why, Mr. Carpentier . . . how you go on.

MR. CARPENTIER
Not at all, my dear Miss Moskowitz . . .

MISS MOSKOWITZ
Call me Madge.

MR. JONES *(Sarcastic)*
I'm sorry to interrupt this . . .

MR. CARPENTIER
A.T. to you . . . A.T. Booker Carpentier at your service.

MR. JONES
. . . This is a college classroom . . . not a French boudoir.

MISS MOSKOWITZ *(To JONES)*
Watch your mouth, young man! There's ladies present.

MARTHA *(To MOSKOWITZ)*
Don't let that bother you, dearie.

LENARD
What kind of attitude must you establish with this type of story and do you create initial attitudes through mood?

MR. JONES *(Confused)*
I beg your pardon?

MR. CARPENTIER *(Answering)*
Why, young man, almost from the beginning the central motif should plant the atmosphere of . . .

MR. JONES
Thank you, Mr. Carpentier!

MR. CARPENTIER
But I wasn't . . .

BILL *(Cutting)*
To what audience is it addressed?

SUE
Good for you!

MISS MOSKOWITZ
Why, young people, of course. In fact, for children.

MR. CARPENTIER
I hardly would think so!

MARTHA
Oh, what kinda stuff is this?

MISS MOSKOWITZ
Mr. Carpentier ... I ...

MR. JONES
Well, at least you're talking about something vaguely dealing with writing. Go on, Mr. Carpentier, try and develop your ...

MR. CARPENTIER
A question of intellectual levels is being probed here ... The question is the adult or the child ... hmm ... *Robinson Crusoe, Gulliver's Travels, Alice in Wonderland, Animal Farm* can all be read by children, dear lady, but the works have added implication for the adult ... in a word, they are potent!

MARTHA
You're talking about universality, man, not audience!

MR. CARPENTIER
Do you know the difference?

LENARD *(Challenges* CARPENTIER)
What's the definition of audience?

MR. CARPENTIER
Of, course, I don't use myself as any type of criteria, but I don't see where that story would appeal to my sophisticated literary tastes, whereas ...

MR. JONES
Now you are quite off the point, Mr. Carpentier.

BILL
He thinks we should all write like the Marquis de Sade.

SUE
Yeah, bedtime tales for tykes by Sade.

MISS MOSKOWITZ
I think you're trying to place an imposition of the adult world on the child's.

THE ELECTRONIC NIGGER   237

MR. JONES
The important thing is to write the story, class. To write the story!

MR. CARPENTIER
Well, I think that the story was not at all that emphatic ... it didn't emote ... it didn't elicite my ...

MISS MOSKOWITZ *(Confused)*
Why didn't it?

MR. CARPENTIER
I don't think the child would have the range of actual patterns for his peer group in this circumstantial instance.

MARTHA
What, man?

LENARD
I got the impression that the protagonists are exempliar.

MR. JONES
Class, do you think this story line aids the writer in performing his functions? ... The culture has values and the writer's duties are to ...

MR. CARPENTIER
No, I don't think this story does it!

SUE
Why not?

MR. CARPENTIER
It is fallacious!

MISS MOSKOWITZ
But it's only a child's story, a fantasy, Mr. Carpentier!

MR. JONES
Yes, a child's story ... for children, man!

MR. CARPENTIER
But it doesn't ring true, dear lady. The only way one can get the naturalistic speech and peer group patterns and mores of children recorded accurately ...

MR. JONES *(begins a string of "Oh God's" rising in volume until* MR. CARPENTIER *finishes his speech)*
Oh God, Oh, God, *Oh, God, Oh, God,* OH, GOD!

MR. CARPENTIER
... is to scientifically eavesdrop on their peer group with electronic listening devices and get the actual evidence for any realistic fictionalizing one wishes to achieve.

MR. JONES *(Scream)*
NO!!!

MR. CARPENTIER *(Query)*
No?

MR. JONES *(In a tired voice)*
Thomas Wolfe once said ...

MR. CARPENTIER *(Ridicule)*
Thomas Wolfe!

MR. JONES
"I believe that we are lost here in America, but I believe we shall be found.".... Mr. Carpentier ... let's hope that we Black Americans can first find ourselves and perhaps be equal to the task ... the burdensome and sometimes evil task, by the way ... that being an American calls for in these days.

MR. CARPENTIER
Sir, I object!

MR. JONES
Does not the writer have some type of obligation to remove some of the intellectual as well as political, moral and social tyranny that infects this culture? What does all the large words in creation serve you, my Black brother, if you are a complete whitewashed man?

MR. CARPENTIER
Sir, I am not black nor your brother ... There is a school of thought that is diametrically opposed to you and your black chauvinism ... You preach bigotry, black nation-

THE ELECTRONIC NIGGER   239

alism, and fascism! . . . The idea . . . black brother . . .
intellectual barbarism! . . . Your statements should be
reported to the school board—as well as your permitting
smoking in your classroom.

SUE
Shut up, you Uncle Tom bastard!

BILL *(Pulls her back)*
That's for me to do, not you, lady!

MR. JONES
Four hundred years. . . . Four hundred . . .

LENARD
We'll picket any attempt to have Mr. Jones removed!

MARTHA *(Disgust)*
This is adult education?

MISS MOSKOWITZ *(To* MR. CARPENTIER)
I bet George Bernard Shaw would have some answers
for you!

MR. CARPENTIER
Of course when examining G. B. Shaw you will discover he is advancing Fabian Socialism.

BILL
Who would picket a vacuum?

LENARD
Your levity escapes me.

SUE
Your what, junior?

MR. JONES
Let's try and go on, class. If you'll . . .

MR. CARPENTIER *(To* MISS MOSKOWITZ)
Your story just isn't professional, miss. It doesn't follow the Hitchcock formula . . . it just doesn't follow . . .

MISS MOSKOWITZ
Do you really think so?

MR. JONES
Somehow, I do now believe that you are quite real, Mr.
Carpentier.

LENARD *(To* MR. CARPENTIER)
Have you read *The Invisible Man?*

BILL
Are you kidding?

MR. CARPENTIER
Socio Drama will be the new breakthrough in the the-
atrical-literary community.

MR. JONES
Oh, Lord . . . not again. This is madness.

MR. CARPENTIER
Combined with the social psychologist's case study, and
the daily experiences of some habitant of a socio-eco-
nomically depressed area, is the genius of the intellectual and artistic craftsman.

MR. JONES
Madness!

MISS MOSKOWITZ
Socio Drama . . . how thrilling.

MR. JONES
Don't listen to him, class . . . I'm the teacher,
understand?

MR. CARPENTIER
Yes, yes . . . let me tell you a not quite unique but never-
theless interesting phenomenon . . .

MR. JONES
Now we know that there is realism, and naturalism
and surrealism . . .

MR. CARPENTIER
. . . an extremely interesting phenomenon . . . adolescent necrophilia!

MARTHA
Oh, shit!

MR. JONES
I have a degree.... I've written a book.... Please don't
listen ...

MISS MOSKOWITZ
It sounds fascinating, Mr. Carpentier.

MR. CARPENTIER
Yes, tramps will freeze to death and kids, children, will
punch holes in the corpses ...

LENARD
Isn't that reaching rather far just to prove that truth
is stranger than fiction?

SUE
I have a story about crud and filth and disease ...

MR. JONES
And stupidity and ignorance and vulgarity and de-
spair ...

MR. CARPENTIER
I go back to my original point ... I go back to necrophilia!

BILL
And loneliness ... and emptiness ... and death.

MR. CARPENTIER
Cadavers! Cadavers! Yes, I come back to that!... Those
findings could almost be case studies of true cases, they
are so true in themselves, and that's where the real truth
lies ... Verily, social case histories of social psycholo-
gists ...

MISS MOSKOWITZ (Enraptured)
Never ... never in all my experience has a class aroused
such passionate response in my life!

LENARD
I don't believe it!

MR. JONES
But I have read Faulkner in his entirety . . .

MR. CARPENTIER
These people in New York, Philadelpha, Boston, Chicago, San Francisco . . . and places like that . . .

MR. JONES
I cut my teeth on Hemingway . . .

MR. CARPENTIER
. . . they just get drunk and die in the streets . . .

MR. JONES
Leaves of Grass is my Bible . . . and Emily Dickinson . . .

MR. CARPENTIER
. . . and then they are prone to suffer adolescent and urchin necrophilia!

MR. JONES *(Frustrated)*
. . . Emily Dickinson has always been on my shelf beside *Mother Goose.*

MR. CARPENTIER
It's curiosity . . . not a sickness . . . curiosity!

MR. JONES
I don't want much . . . just to learn the meaning of life.

MARTHA
Will you discover it here, Ray?

LENARD
But how can anybody be so sure?

MR. CARPENTIER *(Offhand)*
We happen to own some mortuaries . . . my family, that is . . . and it is our experience that children will disarrange a corpse . . . and if we don't watch them closely . . .

MR. JONES
Booker T. Washington walked barefooted to school! Think of that! Barefooted!

MR. CARPENTIER
Once as a case study in experimental methods I placed a microphone in a cadaver and gave some juvenile necrophilics unwitting access to my tramp.

(*JONES almost doubles over and clutches his stomach; his hands and feet twitch*)

MR. JONES
I'd like to adjourn class early tonight . . . will everyone please go home?

MR. CARPENTIER
What I'm saying is this . . . with our present cybernetic generation it is psycho-politically relevant to engage our socio-philosophical existence on a quanitatum scale which is, of course, pertinent to the outer-motivated migration of our inner-oriented social compact. Yes! Yes, indeed, I might add. A most visionary prognosis, as it were, but . . . ha ho ho . . . but we pioneers must look over our bifocals, I always say . . . ha ha ha . . . giving me added insight to perceive the political exiguousness of our true concomitant predicament. True, preclinical preconsciousness gives indication that our trivialization is vulva, but, owing to the press of the press our

LENARD
What's our assignment for next week, Mr. Jones?

MISS MOSKOWITZ
I have something to show you, Mr. Jones.

MARTHA
Are you okay, Mr. Jones?

MR. JONES
Ray . . . just Ray . . . okay?

SUE
Do you have office hours, Mr. Ray?

MR. JONES
I just want everybody to go home now and think about what has happened tonight . . . and if you want to be writers after this then please don't come back to this class.

I've just published an unsuccessful novel, as you know, and I thought I'd avowed aims are maleficent! True! Yes, true! And we are becoming more so. In areas of negative seeming communications probing our error factors are quite negligible. . . . For instance . . . Senator Dodd getting a pension for someone who has gotten abducted and initiated at a Ku Klux meeting . . . well . . . It's poesy! . . . Monochromatic!

teach a while and finish my second one and eat a bit . . . But I think I'd rather not, eat well, that is, so you won't see me next week but if any of you'd like a good steady job I could recommend you . . .

MR. JONES
Reading is the answer. It must be . . . cultivating the sensibilities . . . Plato. . . . Aristotle. . . . Homer. . . . Descartes. . . . And Jones . . . I've always wanted to carry the Jones banner high.

BILL *(To Sue)*
Hey, I've got some pretty good grass that just came in from Mexico.

SUE
Yeah? You have, huh?

BILL
It's at my pad . . . would you like to stop by?

SUE
How far?

BILL
A couple of blocks.

SUE
Okay. It might be interesting.

MR. CARPENTIER *(To a student)*
Ubiquitous! A form of reference which exposes . . .

(BILL *and* SUE *exit. Students begin filing out.* MARTHA *walks over to* MR. JONES, *though the other students are gathered about* MR. CARPENTIER)

MARTHA
You look tired, Ray.

MR. JONES
Yeah . . . yeah . . . I've been reading a lot. The classics are consuming.

MARTHA
Yes, I've heard. Why don't we stop by my place and I'll fix drinks and you can relax . . .

MR. JONES
Okay . . . okay . . . but my ulcer's bothering me . . . Mind if I drink milk?

MARTHA
It's not my stomach.

(She helps him off)

MR. CARPENTIER
Who's that French poet . . . Balu . . .

LENARD
Bouvier?

MR. CARPENTIER
. . . Bali . . . Blau? . . .

(MISS MOSKOWITZ *shows* MR. CARPENTIER *a bound manuscript as he deposits his own in his briefcase)*

MISS MOSKOWITZ
Will you please look at my few labors of love when you find time, Mr. Carpentier?

(He shoves it in the case beside his own)

LENARD *(Gathering his books)*
Mr. Carpentier?

MR. CARPENTIER *(Snapping clasps on his briefcase)*
Yes, Lenard.

LENARD *(Pushing himself between* CARPENTIER
   and other students)
What weight does language have on the contemporary
prevalence to act in existential terms?

MR. CARPENTIER *(Leads them off)*
When the writer first named the crow "Caw Caw" it
was onomatopoeia in practice, of course . . . but too it
became the Egyptian symbol of death.

LENARD
The crow.

   (MISS MOSKOWITZ *giggles.*

   *They all exit crowing: "Caw caw caw caw
   caw . . .")*

                    BLACKNESS

The Electronic Nigger and Others *was transferred off-Broadway to the Martini[*] Theatre where it appeared as* Three Plays by Ed Bullins. *This is a scene fr[ ] Clara's Ole Man. (Photo by Martha Holmes, courtesy of The American Pl[ ] Theatre.)*

CLARA'S OLE MAN

A Play of Lost Innocence

Clara's Ole Man was first performed at the Firehouse Repertory Theater in San Francisco on August 5th, 1965. It was produced by the San Francisco Drama Circle and directed by Robert Hartman. The sets were designed by Louie Gelwicks and Peter Rounds, and the lighting by Verne Shreve. The cast was as follows:

CLARA	Blanche Richardson
BIG GIRL	Margo Norman
JACK	James Robinson
BABY GIRL	Dorothy Parrish
MISS FAMIE	Marie Bell
STOOGIE	Doyle Richmond
BAMA	Roy Hammond
HOSS	Ray Ashby
C. C.	Jerry Kemp

CLARA, a light brown girl of eighteen, well built with long, dark hair. A blond streak runs down the middle of her head, and she affects a pony tail. She is pensive, slow in speech but feline. Her eyes are heavy-lidded and brown; she smiles—rather, blushes—often.

BIG GIRL, a stocky woman wearing jeans and tennis shoes and a tight-fitting blouse which accents her prominent breasts. She is of an indeterminable age, due partly to her lack of make-up and plain hair style. She is anywhere from 25 to 40, and is loud and jolly, frequently breaking out in laughter from her own jokes.

JACK, 20 years old, wears a corduroy Ivy League suit and vest. At first, JACK's speech is modulated and too eloquent for the surroundings, but as he drinks his words become slurred and mumbled.

BABY GIRL, BIG GIRL's mentally retarded teen-age sister. The girl has the exact hairdo as CLARA.

Her face is made up with mascara and eye shadow, and she has black arching eyebrows penciled darkly, the same as CLARA.

MISS FAMIE, a drunken neighbor.

STOOGIE, a local streetfighter and gang leader. His hair is processed.

BAMA, one of STOOGIE's boys.

HOSS, another of STOOGIE's boys.

C.C., a young wino.

Time: Early spring, the mid-1950's.

Scene: A slum kitchen on a rainy afternoon in South Philadelphia. The room is very clean, wax glosses the linoleum and old wooden furniture; a cheap but clean red checkered oilcloth covers the table. If the room could speak it would say, "I'm cheap but clean."

A cheap AM radio plays rhythm 'n' blues music throughout the play. The furniture is made up of a wide kitchen table where a gallon jug of red wine sits. Also upon the table is an oatmeal box, cups, mugs, plates and spoons, ashtrays, and packs of cigarettes. Four chairs circle the table, and two sit against the wall at the back of the stage. An old-fashioned wood- and coal-burning stove takes up a corner of the room and a gas range of 1935 vintage is at the back next to the door to the yard. A large, smoking frying pan is on one of the burners.

JACK and BIG GIRL are seated at opposite ends of the table; CLARA stands at the stove fanning the fumes toward the door. BABY GIRL plays upon the floor with a homemade toy.

CLARA *(Fans fumes)*
Uummm uummm . . . well, there goes the lunch. I wonder how I was dumb enough to burn the bacon?

BIG GIRL
Just comes natural with you, honey, all looks and no brains . . . now with me and my looks, anybody in South Philly can tell I'm a person that naturally takes care of business . . . hee hee . . . ain't that right, Clara?

CLARA
Awww girl, go on. You's the worst messer'upper I knows. You didn't even go to work this mornin'. What kind of business is that?

BIG GIRL
It's all part of my master plan, baby. Don't you worry none . . . Big Girl knows what she's doin'. You better believe that!

CLARA
Yeah, you may know what you're doin' but I'm the one who's got to call in for you and lie that you're sick.

BIG GIRL
Well, it ain't a lie. You know I got this cough and stopped-up feeling.
(Looking at JACK)
You believe that, don't you, youngblood?

JACK
Most certainly. You could very well have a respiratory condition and also have all the appearances of an extremely capable person.

BIG GIRL *(Slapping table)*
Hee hee . . . *See* Clara? . . . *See?* Listen ta that, Clara. I told you anybody could tell it. Even ole hot lips here can tell.

CLARA *(Pours out grease and wipes stove)*
Awww . . . he just says that to be nice . . . he's always sayin' things like that.

BIG GIRL
Is that how he talked when he met you the other day out to your aunt's house?

CLARA *(Hesitating)*
Nawh . . . nawh he didn't talk like that.

BIG GIRL
Well, how did he talk, huh?

CLARA
Awww . . . Big Girl. I don't know.

BIG GIRL
Well, who else does? You know what kind of line a guy gives ya. You been pitched at enough times, haven't ya? By the looks of him I bet he gave ya the ole smooth college boy approach . . .
    (To JACK*)*
C'mon, man, drink up. We got a whole lot mo' to kill. Don't you know this is my day off and I'm celebratin'?

JACK *(Takes a drink)*
Thanks . . . this is certainly nice of you to go to all this trouble for me. I never expected it.

BIG GIRL
What did you expect, youngblood?

JACK *(Takes another sip)*
Ohhh, well . . . I . . .

CLARA *(To* BABY GIRL *on floor)*
Don't put that dirty thing in your mouf, gal!
    (She walks around the table to BABY GIRL *and
    tugs her arm)*
Now, keep that out of your mouf!

BABY GIRL *(Holds to toy sullenly)*
No!

CLARA
You keep quiet, you hear, gal!

BABY GIRL
No ! ! !

CLARA
If you keep tellin' me no I'm goin' ta take you upstairs ta Aunt Toohey.

BABY GIRL *(Throws back head and drums feet on floor)*
NO! NO! SHIT! DAMN! SHIT! NO!

CLARA *(Disturbed)*
Now stop that! We got company.

BIG GIRL *(Laughs hard and leans elbows upon table)*
Haw Haw Haw . . . I guess she told you, Clara. Hee
hee . . . that little dirty mouf bitch
        (Pointing to BABY GIRL *and becoming choked)*
. . . that little . . . cough cough . . . hoooeee, boy!

CLARA
You shouldn't have taught her all them nasty words,
Big Girl. Now we can't do anything with her.
        (Turns to JACK)
What do you think of that?

JACK
Yes, it does seem a problem. But with proper guidance
she'll more than likely be conditioned out of it when
she gets into a learning situation among her peer
group.

BIG GIRL *(Takes a drink and scowls)*
Bullshit!

CLARA
Awww . . . B.G.

JACK
I beg your pardon, Miss?

BIG GIRL
I said bullshit! Whatta ya mean with proper guidance . . .
        (Points)
I taught that little bitch myself . . . the best cuss
words I know before she ever climbed out of her crib
. . . whatta ya mean when she gets among her "peer
group"?

JACK
I didn't exactly say that. I said when . . .

BIG GIRL *(Cuts him off)*
Don't tell me what you said, boy! I got ears. I know

all them big horseshit doctor words . . . tell him, Clara
. . . tell him what I do. Where do I work, Clara?

CLARA
Awww . . . B.G., please.

BIG GIRL
DO LIKE I SAY! DO LIKE BIG WANTS YOU TO!

CLARA *(Surrenders)*
She works out at the state nut farm.

BIG GIRL *(Triumphant)*
And tell mister smart and proper what I do.

CLARA *(Automatically)*
She's a technician.

JACK
Oh, that's nice. I didn't mean to suggest there was
anything wrong with how you raised your sister.

BIG GIRL *(Jolly again)*
Haw haw haw . . . Nawh, ya didn't. I know you didn't
even know what you were sayin', youngblood. Do you
know why I taught her to cuss?

JACK
Why no, I have no idea. Why did you?

BIG GIRL
Well, it was to give her freedom, ya know?

(JACK *shakes his head*)

Ya see workin' in the hospital with all the nuts and
fruits and crazies and weirdos I get ideas 'bout things.
I saw how when they get these kids in who have
cracked up and even with older people who come in
out of their skulls they all mostly cuss. Mostly all of
them, all the time they out of their heads, they cuss all
the time and do other wild things, and boy do some of
them really get into it and let out all of that filthy shit
that's been stored up all them years. But when the docs
start shockin' them and puttin' them on insulin they

quiets down, that's when the docs think they're gettin' better, but really they ain't. They're just learn'n like before to hold it in . . . just like before, that's one reason most of them come back or are always on the verge afterwards of goin' psycho again.

JACK *(Enthusiastic)*
Wow, I never thought of that! That ritual action of purging and catharsis can open up new avenues of therapy and in learning theory and conditioning subjects . . .

BIG GIRL
Saaay whaaa . . . ? What did you have for breakfast, man?

CLARA *(Struck)*
That sounds so wonderful . . .

JACK *(Still excited)*
But I agree with you. You have an intuitive grasp of very abstract concepts!

BIG GIRL *(Beaming)*
Yeah, yeah . . . I got a lot of it figured out . . .
    (To JACK)
Here, fill up your glass again, man.

JACK *(To* CLARA)
Aren't you drinking with us?

CLARA
Later. Big Girl doesn't allow me to start in drinking too early.

JACK *(Confused)*
She doesn't?

BIG GIRL *(Cuts in)*
Well, in Baby Girl's case I said to myself that I'm teach'n her how in front and lettin' her use what she knows whenever it builds up inside. And it's really good for her, gives her spirit and everything.

CLARA
That's probably what warped her brain.

BIG GIRL
Hush up! You knows it was dat fuckin' disease. All the doctors said so.

CLARA
You don't believe no doctors 'bout nothin' else!

BIG GIRL *(Glares at* CLARA*)*
Are you showin' out, Clara? Are you showin' out to your little boyfriend?

CLARA
He ain't mah boyfriend.

JACK *(Interrupts)*
How do you know she might not have spirit if she wasn't allowed to curse?

BIG GIRL *(Sullen)*
I don't know anything, youngblood. But I can take a look at myself and see the two of us. Look at me!
     (Stares at JACK*)*
LOOK AT ME!

JACK
Yes, yes, I'm looking.

BIG GIRL
Well, what do you see?

CLARA
B.G. . . . *please!*

BIG GIRL *(Ignores)*
Well, what do you see?

JACK *(Worried)*
Well, I don't really know . . . I . . .

BIG GIRL
Well, let me tell you what you see. You see a fat bitch who's twenty pounds overweight and looks ten years years older than she is. You want to know how I got

this way and been this way most of my life and would be worse off if I didn't let off steam some drinkin' this rotgut and speakin' my mind?

JACK *(To* BIG GIRL *who doesn't listen but drinks)*
Yes, I would like to hear.

> (CLARA *finishes the stove and takes a seat between the two.* BABY GIRL *goes to the yard door but does not go out into the rain; she sits down and looks out through the door at an angle)*

BIG GIRL
Ya see, when I was a little runt of a kid my mother found out she couldn't keep me or Baby Girl any longer cause she had T.B., so I got shipped out somewheres and Baby Girl got shipped out somewheres else. People that Baby Girl went to exposed her to the disease. She was lucky. I ended up with some fuckin' Christians . . .

CLARA
Ohhh, B.G., you shouldn't say that!

BIG GIRL
Well, I sho as hell just did! . . . Damned kristers! I spent twelve years with those people, can you imagine? A dozen years in hell. Christians . . . *haaa* . . . always preachin' bout some heaven over yonder and building a bigger hell here den any devil have imagination for.

CLARA
You shouldn't go round sayin' things like dat.

BIG GIRL
I shouldn't! Well, what did your Christian mammy and pot-gutted pappy teach you? When I met you you didn't even know how to take a douche.

CLARA
YOU GOT NO RIGHT ! ! !
> *(She momentarily rises as if she's going to launch herself on* BIG GIRL)*

CLARA'S OLE MAN   259

BIG GIRL *(Condescending)*
Awww . . . forget it, sweetie . . . don't make no never mind, but you remember how you us'ta smell when you got ready fo bed . . . like a dead hoss or a baby skunk . . .
(To JACK, *explaining)*
That damned Christian mamma and pappa of hers didn't tell her a thing 'bout herself . . . ha ha ha . . . thought if she ever found out her little things was used fo anything else 'cept squattin' she'd fall backwards right up in it . . . ZaaaBOOM . . . STRAIGHT TA HELL . . . ha ha . . . didn't know that li'l Clara had already found her heaven, and on the same trail.

CLARA *(Ashamed)*
Sometimes . . . sometimes . . . I just want to die for bein' here.

BIG GIRL *(Enjoying herself)*
Ha ha ha . . . that wouldn't do no good. Would it? Just remember what shape you were in when I met you, kid. Ha ha ha.
(To JACK)
Hey, boy, can you imagine this pretty little trick here had her stomach seven months in the wind, waitin' on a dead baby who died from the same disease that Baby Girl had . . .

CLARA
He didn't have any nasty disease like Baby Girl!

BABY GIRL *(Hears her name but looks out door)*
NO! NO! SHIT! DAMN! SHIT! SHIT!

BIG GIRL
Haw haw haw . . . Now we got her started . . .
(She laughs for over a minute; JACK waits patiently, sipping; CLARA is grim. BABY GIRL has quieted)

She . . . she . . . ha ha . . . was walkin' round with a dead baby in her and had no place to go.

CLARA *(Fills a glass)*

I just can't understand you, B.G. You know my baby died after he was born. Some days you just get besides yourself.

BIG GIRL

I'm only helpin' ya entertain your guest.

CLARA

Awww . . . B.G. It wasn't his fault. I invited him.

JACK *(Dismayed)*

Well, I asked really. If there's anything wrong I can go.

BIG GIRL

Take it easy, youngblood. I'm just havin' a little fun. Now let's get back to the Clara Saga . . . ya hear that word, junior? . . . S-A-G-A, SUCKER! You college boys don't know it all. Yeah, her folks had kicked her out and the little punk she was big for what had tried to put her out on the block and when that didn't work out . . .
   (Mocking and making pretended blushes)
because our sweet little thing here was soooo modest and sedate . . . the nigger split! . . . HAW HAW HAW . . . HE MADE IT TO NEW YORK!
   (She goes into a laughing, choking and crying fit. BABY GIRL rushes over to her and on tiptoe pats her back)

BABY GIRL

Big Girl! Big Girl! Big Girl!

   (A knocking sounds and CLARA exits to answer the door)

BIG GIRL *(Catches her breath)*

Whatcha want, little sister?

BABY GIRL

The cat! The cat! It's got some kittens! The cat got some kittens!

BIG GIRL *(Still coughing and choking)*
Awww, go on. You know there ain't no cats under there with no kittens.
>*(To* JACK)

She's been makin' that story up for two months now about how some cat crawls up under the steps and has kittens. She can't fool me none. She just wants a cat but I ain't gonna get none.

JACK
Why not? Cats aren't so bad. My mother has one and he's quite a pleasure to her.

BIG GIRL
For your mammy maybe, but all they mean round here
>*(Singsong)*

is fleas and mo' mouths to feed. With an invalid aunt upstairs we don't need any mo' expenses.

JACK *(Gestures toward* BABY GIRL)
It shows that she has a very vivid imagination to make up that story about the kittens.

BIG GIRL
Yeah, her big sister ain't the biggest liar in the family.

>(CLARA *returns with* MISS FAMIE *staggering behind her, a thin middle-aged woman in long seamen's raincoat, dripping wet, and wearing house slippers that are soaked and squish water about the kitchen floor)*

BIG GIRL
Hi, Miss Famie. I see you're dressed in your rainy glad rags today.

MISS FAMIE *(Slurred speech of the drunk)*
Hello, B.G. Yeah, I couldn't pass up seein' Aunt Toohey, so I put on my weather coat. You know that don't a day pass that I don't stop up to see her.

BIG GIRL
Yeah, I know, Miss Famie. Every day you go up there

with that quart of gin under your dress and you two ole lushes put it away.

MISS FAMIE
Why, B.G. You should know better than that.

CLARA *(Re-seated)*
B.G., you shouldn't say that . . .

BIG GIRL
Why shouldn't I? I'm payin' for over half of that juice and I don't git to see none of it 'cept the empty bottles.

BABY GIRL
CAT! CAT! CAT!

MISS FAMIE
Oh, the baby still sees them there cats.

CLARA
You should be ashamed to talk to Miss Famie like that.

BIG GIRL *(To JACK)*
Why you so quiet? Can't you speak to folks when they come in?

JACK
I'm sorry.
          (To MISS FAMIE)
Hello, ma'am.

MISS FAMIE
Why howdie, son.

CLARA
Would you like a glass of wine, Miss Famie?

MISS FAMIE
Don't mind if I do, sister.

BIG GIRL
Better watch it, Miss Famie. Wine and gin will rust your gizzard.

CLARA
Ohhh . . .

(Pours a glass of wine)
. . . Here, Miss Famie.

BABY GIRL
CAT! CAT!

BIG GIRL *(Singsong, lifting her glass)*
Mus' I tell' . . . *muscatel* . . . jitterbug champagne.
(Reminisces)
Remember, Clara, the first time I got you to take a
drink?
(To MISS FAMIE*)*
You should of seen her. Some of this same cheap rotgut here. She'd never had a drink before but she
wanted to show me how game she was. She was a
bright little smart thing, just out of high school and
didn't know her butt from a door knob.

MISS FAMIE
Yes, indeed, that was Clara all right.

BIG GIRL
She drank three waterglasses down and got so damned
sick I had to put my finger down her throat and make
her heave it up . . . HAW HAW . . . babbled her fool
head off all night . . . said she'd be my friend always
. . . that we'd always be together . . .

MISS FAMIE *(Gulps down her drink)*
Wine will make you do that the first time you get
good 'n high on it.

JACK *(Takes a drink)*
I don't know. You know . . . I've never really been
wasted and I've been drinkin' for quite some time now.

BIG GIRL
Quite some time, huh? How long? Six months?

JACK
Nawh. My mother used to let me drink at home. I've
been drinkin' since fifteen. And I drank all the
time I was in the service.

BIG GIRL

Just because you been slippin' some drinks out of ya mammy's bottle and you slipped a few under ya belt with the punks in the barracks don't make ya a drinker, boy!

CLARA

B.G. . . . do you have to?

> (MISS FAMIE *finishes her second drink as* BIG GIRL *and* CLARA *stare at each other*)

MISS FAMIE

Well, I guess I better get up and see Aunt Toohey.
> *(She leaves)*

BIG GIRL *(Before* MISS FAMIE *reaches top of stairs)*

That ole ginhead tracked water all over your floor, Clara.

CLARA

Makes no never mind to me. This place stays so clean I like when someone comes so it gets a little messy so I have somethin' ta do.

BIG GIRL

Is that why Jackie boy is here? So he can do some messin' 'round?

CLARA

Nawh, B.G.

JACK *(Stands)*

Well, I'll be going. I see that . . .

BIG GIRL *(Rises and tugs his sleeve)*

Sit down an' drink up, youngblood.
> *(Pushes him back into his seat)*

There's wine here . . .
> *(Slow and suggestive)*

. . . there's a pretty girl here . . . you go for that, don't you?

JACK

It's not that . . .

BIG GIRL
You go for fine little Clara, don't you?

JACK
Well, yes, I do . . .

BIG GIRL
HAW HAW HAW . . .
(Slams the table and sloshes wine)
. . . HAW HAW HAW . . .
(Slow and suggestive)
. . . What I tell ya, Clara? You're a winner. First time
I laid eyes on you I said to myself that you's a winner.

CLARA *(Takes a drink)*
Drink up, B.G.

BIG GIRL *(To* JACK)
You sho you like what you see, youngblood?

JACK *(Becomes bold)*
Why, sure. Do you think I'd come out on a day like
this for anybody?

BIG GIRL
HAW HAW HAW . . .
(Peals of laughter and more coughs)

JACK *(To* CLARA)
I was going to ask you to go to the matinee 'round
Pep's, but I guess it's too late now.

CLARA *(Hesitates)*
I never been.

BIG GIRL *(Sobers)*
That's right. You never been to Pep's and it's only
'round the corner. What you mean it's too late, youngblood? It don't start gettin' good till 'round four.

JACK
I thought she might have ta start gettin' supper.

BIG GIRL
She'd only burn it the fuck up too if she did.

(*To* CLARA)
I'm goin' ta take you to Pep's this afternoon.

CLARA
You don't have ta, B.G.

BIG GIRL
It's my day off, ain't it?

CLARA
But it costs so much, don't it?

BIG GIRL
Nawh, not much . . . you'll like it. Soon as C.C. comes over to watch Baby Girl we can go.

CLARA (*Brightens*)
O.K.!

JACK
I don't know who's there now, but they always have a good show. Sometimes Ahmad Jamal . . .

BABY GIRL (*Cuts speech*)
CAT! CAT! CAT!

BIG GIRL
Let's toast to that . . .
        (*Raising her glass*)
. . . To Pep's on a rainy day!

JACK
HERE HERE!
        (*He drains his glass.*

        A tumbling sound is heard from the backyard as they drink and BABY GIRL *claps hands as* STOOGIE, BAMA, *and* HOSS *appear in yard doorway. The three boys are no more than sixteen. They are soaked but wear only thin jackets, caps and pants. Under* STOOGIE's *cap he wears a bandanna to keep his processed hair dry*)

BIG GIRL
What the hell is this?

STOOGIE *(Goes to* BIG GIRL *and pats her shoulder)*
The heat, B. G. The man was on our asses so we had to come on in out of the rain, baby, dig?

BIG GIRL
Well, tell me somethin' I don't know, baby. Why you got to pick mah back door? I ain't never ready for any more heat than I gets already.

STOOGIE
It just happened that way, B.G. We didn't have any choice.

BAMA
That's right, Big Girl. You know we ain't lame 'nuf to be usin' yo pad fo no highway.

HOSS
Yeah, baby, you know how it is when the man is there.

BIG GIRL
Well, what makes a difference . . .
        (Smiles)
. . . Hey, what'cha standin' there with your faces hangin' out for? Get yourselves a drink.

        (HOSS *goes to the sink to get glasses for the*
        trio: STOOGIE *looks* JACK *over and nods to*
        BAMA, *then turns to* CLARA)

STOOGIE
How ya doin', Clara? Ya lookin' fine as ever.

CLARA
I'm okay, Stoogie. I don't have to ask 'bout you none. Bad news sho' travels fast.

STOOGIE *(Holds arms apart in innocence)*
What'cha mean, baby? What'cha been hearin' bout poppa Stoogie?

CLARA
Just the regular. That your gang's fightin' the Peaceful Valley guys up in North Philly.

STOOGIE
Awww ... dat's old stuff. Sheeet ... you way behind, baby.

BAMA
Yeah, sweetcake, dat's over.

CLARA
Already?

HOSS
Yeah, we just finished sign'n' a peace treaty with Peaceful Valley.

BAMA
Yeah, we out ta cool the War Lords now from ov'va on Powelton Avenue.

HOSS
Ole Stoogie here is settin' up the war council now; we got a pact with Peaceful Valley and man, when we come down on those punk War Lords ... baby ... it's just gonna be all ov'va.

BIG GIRL
Yeah, it's always one thing ta another with you punks.

STOOGIE
Hey, B.G., cool it! We can't help it if people always spreadin' rumors 'bout us. Things just happen an' people talk and don' understand and get it all wrong, dat's all.

BIG GIRL
Yeah, all of it just happens, huh? It's just natural ... you's growin' boys.

STOOGIE
That's what's happen'n, baby. Now take for instance Peaceful Valley. Las' week we went up there ... ya know, only five of us in Crook's Buick.

CLARA
I guess ya was just lookin' at the scenery?

STOOGIE

Yeah, baby, dat's it. We was lookin' . . . lookin' fo' some jive half-ass niggers.

(The boys laugh and giggle as STOOGIE *enacts the story)*

STOOGIE

Yeah, we spot Specs from offa Jefferson and Gratz walkin' with them bad foots down Master . . . ha ha ha . . .

BAMA

Tell them what happened to Specs, man.

HOSS

Awww, man, ya ain't gonna drag mah man Bama again?

(They laugh more, slapping and punching each other, taking off their caps and cracking each other with them, gulping their wine and performing for the girls and JACK. STOOGIE *has his hair exposed)*

STOOGIE

Bama here . . . ha ha ha . . . Bama burnt dat four-eyed mathafukker in the leg.

HOSS

Baby, you shoulda seen it!

CLARA

Yeah, that's what I heard.

STOOGIE

Yeah, but listen, baby.
(Points to BAMA)
He was holding the only heat we had . . . ha ho ho . . . and dis jive sucker was aimin' at Specs' bad foots . . . ha ha . . . while that blind mathafukker was blastin' from round the corner straight through the car window . . .

(They become nearly hysterical with laughter and stagger and stumble around the table)

HOSS
Yeah . . . ha ha . . . mathafukkin' glass was flyin' all over us . . . ha ha . . . we almost got sliced ta death and dis stupid mathafukker was shootin' at the man's bad foots . . . ha ha . . .

BAMA *(Scratching his head)*
Well, man. Well, man . . . I didn't know what kind of rumble we was in.

> *(CLARA and BIG GIRL laugh as they refill their glasses, nearly emptying the jug. BIG GIRL gets up and from out of the refrigerator pulls another gallon as laughter subsides)*

BIG GIRL *(Sits down)*
What's the heat doin' after ya?

STOOGIE
Nothin'.

CLARA
I bet!

STOOGIE *(Sneer)*
That's right, baby. They just singled us out to make examples of.
> *(This gets a laugh from his friends)*

BIG GIRL
What did you get?

HOSS
Get?

BIG GIRL *(Turns on him)*
You tryin' ta get wise, punk?

STOOGIE *(Patronizing)*
Awww, B.G. You not goin' ta take us serious, are ya?
> *(Silence)*

CLARA'S OLE MAN   271

Well, ya see. We were walkin' down Broad Street by the State Store, see? And we see this old rumdum come out and stagger down the street carryin' this heavy package ...

CLARA
And? ...

STOOGIE
And he's stumblin', see. Like he's gonna fall. So good ole Hoss here says, "Why don't we help that pore man out?" So Bama walks up and helps the man carry his package, and do you know what?

BIG GIRL
Yeah, the mathafukker "slips" down and screams and some cops think you some wrongdoin' studs ... yeah, I know ... of course you didn't have time to explain.

STOOGIE
That's right, B.G. So to get our breath so we could tell our side of it we just stepped in here, dig?

BIG GIRL
Yeah, I dig.
        (Menacing)
Where is it?

HOSS
Where's what?

        (Silence)

STOOGIE
If you had just give me another minute, B.G.
        (Pulls out a quart of vodka)
Well, no use savin' it anyway. Who wants some hundred proof tiger piss?

BAMA *(To STOOGIE)*
Hey, man, how much was in dat mathafukker's wallet?

STOOGIE *(Nods toward JACK)*
Cool it, sucker.

HOSS *(To* STOOGIE)
But, man, you holdin' the watch and ring too!

STOOGIE *(Advancing on them)*
What's wrong with you jive-ass mathafukkers?

BIG GIRL
Okay, cool it! There's only one person gets out of hand
'round here, ya understand?

STOOGIE
Okay, B.G. Let it slide . . .

BABY GIRL
CAT! CAT! CAT!

STOOGIE *(To* JACK)
Drink up, man. Not every day ya get dis stuff.

> (BAMA *picks up the beat of the music and be-
> gins a shuffling dance.* BABY GIRL *begins
> bouncing in time to the music)*

HOSS
C'mon, Baby Girl; let me see ya do the slide.

BABY GIRL
NO! NO!
(She claps and bounces)

HOSS *(Demonstrates his steps, trying to outdance*
BAMA)
C'mon, Baby Girl, shake that thing!

CLARA
No, stop that, Hoss. She don't know what she's doin'.

BIG GIRL
That's okay, Clara. Go on, Baby Girl, do the thing.

> (STOOGIE *grabs salt from the table and shakes
> it upon the floor, under the feet of the dancers)*

STOOGIE
DO THE SLIDE, MAN! SLIDE!

(BABY GIRL *lumbers up and begins a grotesque maneuver while grunting out strained sounds*)

BABY GIRL
Uuuhhhhh . . . sheeeee . . . waaaa . . . uuhhhh . . .

BIG GIRL *(Standing, toasting)*
DO THE THING, BABY ! ! ! !

CLARA
Awww . . . B.G. Why don' you stop all dat?

STOOGIE *(To* JACK)
C'mon, man, git with it.

(JACK *shakes his head and* STOOGIE *goes over to* CLARA *and holds out his hand*)

STOOGIE
Let's go, baby.

CLARA
Nawh . . . I don't dance no mo' . . .

STOOGIE
C'mon, pretty mamma . . . watch this step . . .
(He cuts a fancy step)

BIG GIRL
Go on and dance, sister.

(STOOGIE *moves off and the three boys dance*)

CLARA
Nawh . . . B.G., you know I don't go for that kind of stuff no mo'.

BIG GIRL
Go on, baby!

CLARA
No!

BIG GIRL
I want you to dance, Clara.

CLARA
Nawh . . . I just can't.

BIG GIRL
DO LIKE I SAY! DO LIKE BIG WANTS!

> (*The dancers stop momentarily but begin again when* CLARA *joins them.* BABY GIRL *halts and resumes her place upon the floor, fondling her toy. The others dance until the record stops*)

STOOGIE (*To* JACK)
Where you from, man?

JACK
Oh, I live over in West Philly now, but I come from up around Master.

STOOGIE
Oh? Do you know Hector?

JACK (*Trying to capture an old voice and mannerism*)
Yeah, man. I know the cat.

STOOGIE
What's your name, man?

JACK
Jack, man. Maybe you know me by Tookie.

STOOGIE (*Ritually*)
Tookie . . . Tookie . . . yeah, man, I think I heard about you. You us'ta be in the ole Jet Cobras!

JACK
Well, I us'ta know some of the guys then. I been away for a while.

BAMA (*Matter-of-factly*)
Where you been, man? Jail?

JACK
I was in the marines for three years.

STOOGIE
Hey, man. That must'a been a gas.

JACK
It was okay. I seen a lot . . . went a lot of places.

BIG GIRL
Yeah, you must'a seen it all.

STOOGIE
Did you get to go anywhere overseas, man?

JACK
Yeah, I was aboard ship most of the time.

HOSS
Wow, man. That sounds cool.

BAMA
You really was overseas, man?

JACK
Yeah. I went to Europe and North Africa and the
Caribbean.

STOOGIE
What kind of boat were you on, man?

JACK
A ship.

BIG GIRL
A boat!

JACK
No, a ship.

STOOGIE *(Rising,* BAMA *and* HOSS *surrounding*
    JACK)
Yeah, man, dat's what she said . . . a boat!

CLARA
STOP IT ! ! !

BABY GIRL
NO! NO! NO! SHIT! SHIT! SHIT! DAMN! SHIT!

MISS FAMIE'S VOICE *(From upstairs)*
Your aunt don't like all that noise.

BIG GIRL
You and my aunt better mind ya fukkin' ginhead business or I'll come up there and ram those empty bottles up where it counts!

BAMA *(Sniggling)*
Oh, baby. We forgot your aunt was up dere sick.

STOOGIE
Yeah, baby. Have another drink.
> *(He fills all glasses except CLARA's; she pulls hers away)*

CLARA
Nawh, I don't want any more. Me and Big Girl are goin' out after a while.

BAMA
Can I go too?

BIG GIRL
There's always have ta be one wise mathafukker.

BAMA
I didn't mean nuttin', B.G., honest.

STOOGIE *(To JACK)*
What did you do in the army, man?

JACK *(Feigns a dialect)*
Ohhh, man. I told you already I was in the marines!

HOSS *(To CLARA)*
Where you goin'?

CLARA
B.G.'s takin' me to Pep's.

BAMA
Wow . . . dat's nice, baby.

BIG GIRL *(Gesturing toward JACK)*
Ole smoothie here suggested takin' Clara but it seems he backed out, so I thought we might step around there anyway.

JACK *(Annoyed)*
I didn't back out!

STOOGIE *(To* JACK)
Did you screw any of them foreign bitches when you were in Japan, man?

JACK
Yeah man. I couldn't help it. They were all over, ya know?

BIG GIRL
He couldn't beat them off.

STOOGIE
Yeah, man. I dig.

JACK
Especially in France and Italy. Course, the Spanish girls are the best, but the ones in France and Italy ain't so bad either.

HOSS
You mean those French girls ain't as good as those Spanish girls?

JACK
Nawh, man, the Spanish girls are the best.

BAMA
I never did dig no Mexican nor Rican spic bitches too tough, man.

JACK
They ain't Mexican or Puerto Rican. They Spanish . . . from Spain . . . Spanish is different from Mexican. In Spain . . .

STOOGIE
Whatcha do now, man?

JACK
Ohhh . . . I'm goin' ta college prep on the G.I. Bill now . . . and workin' a little.

STOOGIE
Is that why you sound like you got a load of shit in your mouth?

JACK
What do you mean!

STOOGIE
I thought you talked like you had shit in your mouth because you been ta college, man.

JACK
I don't understand what you're trying ta say, man.

STOOGIE
It's nothin', man. You just talk funny sometimes . . . ya know what I mean. Hey, man, where do you work?

JACK (*Visibly feeling his drinks*)
Nawh, man, I don't know what ya mean, and I don't go to college, man, it's college prep.

STOOGIE
Thanks, man.

JACK
And I work at the P.O.

BAMA
Pee-who?

JACK
The Post Office, man.

STOOGIE
Thanks, George. I always like to know things I don't know anything about.
    (*He turns his back on* JACK)

JACK (*To* BIG GIRL)
Hey, what time ya goin' round to Pep's?

BIG GIRL
Soon . . . are you in a hurry, youngblood? You don't have to wait for us.

JACK *(Now drunk)*
That's okay . . . It's just gettin' late, ya know, man . . .
and I was wonderin' what time Clara's ole man gets
home . . .

BIG GIRL
Clara's ole man? . . . What do you mean, man? . . .

> *(The trio begins snickering, holding their laugh-
> ter back; JACK is too drunk to notice)*

JACK
Well, Clara said for me to come by today in the afternoon when her ole man would be at work . . . and I was
wonderin' what time he got home . . .

> *(BIG GIRL stands, tilting over her chair to
> crash backwards on the floor. Her bust juts out;
> she is controlled but furious)*

BIG GIRL
Clara's ole man is home now . . .

> *(A noise is heard outside as C.C. comes in the
> front door. The trio are laughing louder but with
> restraint; CLARA looks stunned)*

JACK *(Starts up and feels drunk for the first time)*
Wha . . . you mean he's been upstairs all this time?

BIG GIRL *(Staring)*
Nawh, man, I don't mean that!

JACK *(Looks at BIG GIRL, then at the laughing boys
and finally to CLARA)*
Ohhh . . . jeezus!
> *(He staggers to the backyard door, past BABY
> GIRL, and becomes sick)*

BIG GIRL
Didn't you tell him? Didn't you tell him a fukkin'
thing?

> *(C.C. comes in. He is drunk and weaves and says
> nothing. He sees the wine, searches for a glass,*

bumps into one of the boys, is shoved into an-
other, and gets booted in the rear before he
reaches wine and seat)

BIG GIRL
Didn't you tell him?

CLARA
I only wanted to talk, B.G. I only wanted to talk to
somebody. I don't have anybody to talk to . . .
(Crying)
. . . I don't have anyone . . .

BIG GIRL
It's time for the matinee.
(To STOOGIE)
Before you go, escort my friend out, will ya?

CLARA
Ohhh . . . B.G. I'll do anything but please . . . ohhh Big
. . . I won't forget my promise.

BIG GIRL
Let's go. We don't want to miss the show, do we?

CLARA
Please, B.G., please. Not that. It's not his fault!
Please!

BIG GIRL
DO LIKE I SAY! DO LIKE I WANT YOU TO DO!

(CLARA *drops her head and rises and exits*
stage right followed by BIG GIRL. STOOGIE
and his boys finish their drinks, stalk and swag-
ger about. BAMA *opens the refrigerator and*
HOSS *takes one long last guzzle)*

BAMA
Hey, Stoogie babe, what about the split?

STOOGIE *(Drunk)*
Later, you square-ass, lame-ass mathafukker!

(HOSS *giggles)*

BABY GIRL
CAT! CAT! CAT!

C.C. *(Seated, drinking)*
Shut up, Baby Girl. Ain't no cats out dere.

(MISS FAMIE *staggers from upstairs*)

MISS FAMIE *(Calling back)*
GOOD NIGHT, TOOHEY. See ya tomorrow.

(With a nod from STOOGIE, BAMA and HOSS take JACK's arms and wrestle him into the yard. The sound of JACK's beating is heard. MISS FAMIE wanders to the yard door, looks out but staggers back from what she sees and continues sprawling toward the exit, stage right)

BABY GIRL
CAT! CAT! CAT!

C.C.
SHUT UP! SHUT ON UP, BABY GIRL! I TOLE YA . . . DERE AIN'T NO CATS OUT DERE!!!

BABY GIRL
NO! DAMN! SHIT! SHIT! DAMN! NO! NO!

(STOOGIE looks over the scene and downs his drink, then saunters outside.

Lights dim out until there is a single soft spot on BABY GIRL's head, turned wistfully toward the yard; then blackness)

CURTAIN